TAME
THE FIRE

Daily Affirmations for the Muslim Soul

Lynnette C. Anderson

Dedication

To my beloved daughter Cja Abdus-Salaam, my awesome son and my five precious grandchildren.

Your light, your lessons, and your love continue to inspire my journey and shape my healing. This work is for you, and because of you.

Table of Contents

Dedication 2

Introduction 4

MONTH 1: LIFE 5

MONTH 2: LOVE 17

MONTH 3: AWARENESS 29

MONTH 4: ACKNOWLEDGEMENT 41

MONTH 5: ACCEPTANCE 53

MONTH 6: FORGIVENESS 65

MONTH 7: UNDERSTANDING 77

MONTH 8: FAITH 89

MONTH 9: TRUST 101

MONTH 10: WORTH 113

MONTH 11: SERVICE 125

MONTH 12: PEACE 137

About the Author 148

Introduction

**In the Name of Allah, the Most Merciful,
the Most Compassionate**

This book was written for the Muslim soul who feels too much and says too little.

For the one who struggles with anger, but knows it's rooted in grief.
For the one who says "I'm fine" when they're breaking.
For the one who wants to feel close to Allah again—but doesn't know where to start.

Tame the Fire is not about suppressing emotion. It's about transforming it.
Rooted in emotional intelligence, Islamic guidance, and daily self-awareness, this book is your companion through anger, control, sadness, self-blame, and the unspoken emotional burdens many of us carry.

With each affirmation, you'll learn to pause before reacting.
To reflect before judging.
And to reconnect—with yourself, your Creator, and your peace.

This is not a textbook. It's a daily practice.
May it help you shift from fire to light—one day, one du'a, one breath at a time.

MONTH 1:

LIFE

*"And We have certainly created man and know
what his soul whispers to him..."*
(Surah Qaf 50:16)

This month, we reclaim life—not just as existence, but as intention.
Let each day draw you closer to who you were created to be.

WEEK 1: Days 1–7

Day 1

Affirmation: I am alive today, and that is proof of Allah's mercy.

There was a time when waking up felt like a burden. But slowly, I began to notice how every breath was a chance—not a punishment. Life doesn't mean perfection; it means potential.

📖 Qur'an: "And it is He who gave you life, then will cause you to die, and then will again give you life." (Surah Al-Hajj 22:66)

🕊️ Dua: Ya Hayy, Ya Qayyum, let me honor the life You've given me by walking in purpose and peace.

Day 2

Affirmation: My anger does not define my character—my choices do.

There were days I thought being angry meant I was broken. But then I remembered even the Prophet (ﷺ) taught us that strength is found in self-restraint, not in outbursts.

📖 Hadith: "The strong is not the one who overcomes people by his strength, but the one who controls himself while in anger." (Sahih al-Bukhari)

🕊️ Dua: Ya Allah, give me strength to respond with wisdom when anger visits my heart.

Day 3

Affirmation: Today, I choose life over survival.

I used to go through the motions—wake up, get through the day, go to sleep angry. But choosing life means choosing to feel, to heal, to seek joy, not just avoid pain.

📖 Qur'an: "And whoever saves one [life]—it is as if he had saved mankind entirely." (Surah Al-Ma'idah 5:32)

🤲 Dua: O Sustainer, teach me to live fully, not just to endure. Let me thrive in Your light.

Day 4

Affirmation: I am not alone in my struggle—Allah sees me.

There were nights I cried alone, thinking no one understood. But Allah is Al-Baseer, the All-Seeing. He knew my pain even when I couldn't put it into words.

📖 Qur'an: "Indeed, my Lord is near and responsive." (Surah Hud 11:61)

🤲 Dua: Ya Rabb, let me feel Your nearness when the world feels far away.

Day 5

Affirmation: My emotions are messengers—not masters.

When anger flared, I used to act without thinking. Now I try to listen first. Anger is a signal—something needs care, not punishment.

📖 Hadith: "When one of you becomes angry while standing, he should sit down. If the anger leaves him, well and good; otherwise, he should lie down." (Abu Dawood)

🤲 Dua: Ya Allah, help me understand my emotions so I may act with insight and integrity.

Day 6

Affirmation: My value is not measured by my past, but by my repentance.

Shaytan whispers, 'Look what you've done.' But Allah reminds me, 'Look how you turned back to Me.'

📖 Qur'an: "Say, O My servants who have transgressed against themselves [by sinning], do not despair of the mercy of Allah." (Surah Az-Zumar 39:53)

🤲 Dua: Ya Tawwab, help me accept Your mercy and walk forward without shame.

Day 7

Affirmation: Peace begins when I trust Allah more than my fears.

Fear used to fuel my rage. I thought control would keep me safe. But true peace came when I started trusting that Allah was already holding what I couldn't.

📖 Qur'an: "And whoever relies upon Allah – then He is sufficient for him." (Surah At-Talaq 65:3)

🤲 Dua: Ya Waliyy, calm my heart and remind me that You are enough.

WEEK 2: Days 8–14

Day 8

Affirmation: I am not the storm—I am the one who survived it.

My anger came from the damage, not the core of who I am. Healing reminded me I am more than what hurt me—I am who made it through.

📖 Qur'an: "Indeed, with hardship comes ease." (Surah Ash-Sharh 94:6)

🤲 Dua: Ya Sabur, help me endure with grace and remember my strength is proof of Your mercy.

Day 9

Affirmation: I am allowed to feel and still be faithful.

Some days I questioned why I felt so broken if I trusted Allah. But feelings are not weakness—they're reminders that I'm alive, human, and still trying.

📖 Hadith: The Prophet (ﷺ) said, "Verily, the eyes shed tears and the heart grieves, but we will not say except what pleases our Lord." (Bukhari & Muslim)

🤲 Dua: Ya Rahman, allow me to feel deeply without shame, and to return to You in every emotion.

Day 10

Affirmation: My anger is not my enemy—it is my invitation to reflect.

I used to run from my anger. But now I pause and ask: what wound is speaking? That's where the healing begins.

📖 Qur'an: "And those who restrain anger and who pardon the people – and Allah loves the doers of good." (Surah Ali 'Imran 3:134)

🤲 Dua: Ya Hakim, grant me wisdom to listen to my anger without being led by it.

Day 11

Affirmation: Healing is not linear—but every breath is progress.

I used to be hard on myself for not being 'over it.' But then I realized: even the Prophet (ﷺ) grieved. Healing is not a race—it's a return.

📖 Qur'an: "So be patient. Indeed, the promise of Allah is truth." (Surah Ar-Rum 30:60)

🤲 Dua: Ya Shafi, heal me in Your time, and let me honor every stage of the journey.

Day 12

Affirmation: I was created with dignity—and no one can take that from me.

People tried to break me, and for a while, I believed them. But Allah says I was created in the best form—and I finally started believing Him instead.

📖 Qur'an: "We have certainly created man in the best of stature." (Surah At-Tin 95:4)

🕊 Dua: Ya Aziz, restore my self-worth and clothe me in the dignity You gave me.

Day 13

Affirmation: Silence is sometimes the loudest act of strength.

I used to think I had to shout to be heard. But there is power in choosing silence—not out of fear, but from peace.

📖 Hadith: "Whoever believes in Allah and the Last Day should speak a good word or remain silent." (Bukhari & Muslim)

🕊 Dua: Ya Latif, help me to speak with purpose and be silent with intention.

Day 14

Affirmation: My heart still works—it just needs care, not shame.

I judged myself for being too angry, too emotional. But my heart wasn't damaged—it was trying to survive. Now, I choose care over criticism.

📖 Qur'an: "Verily in the remembrance of Allah do hearts find rest." (Surah Ar-Ra'd 13:28)

🕊 Dua: Ya Allah, soften my heart and let it beat with faith, not fear.

WEEK 3: Days 15–21

Day 15

Affirmation: I do not have to respond to everything—I am allowed peace.

I used to jump at every insult, every slight. But peace came when I realized silence was an act of strength, not surrender.

📖 Qur'an: "And when the ignorant address them [harshly], they say [words of] peace." (Surah Al-Furqan 25:63)

🕊 Dua: Ya Salam, make peace my instinct and not just my goal.

Day 16

Affirmation: I can speak truth without raising my voice.

In my anger, I thought louder meant stronger. But the Prophet (ﷺ) spoke with calm, and his truth changed the world.

📖 Qur'an: "And speak to him with gentle speech that perhaps he may be reminded or fear [Allah]." (Surah Ta-Ha 20:44)

🕊 Dua: Ya Haqq, let my voice carry truth with gentleness and dignity.

Day 17

Affirmation: I will not let pain become my identity.

I used to introduce myself by my trauma—what happened to me. Now, I choose to introduce myself by my resilience.

📖 Qur'an: "Allah does not burden a soul beyond that it can bear." (Surah Al-Baqarah 2:286)

🕊 Dua: Ya Qadir, help me rise beyond my hurt and remember who I am in Your eyes.

Day 18

Affirmation: I forgive myself for not knowing how to heal sooner.

I stayed stuck for so long. But now I realize I needed time, lessons, and mercy—just like everyone else.

📖 Hadith: "All the sons of Adam are sinners, but the best of sinners are those who repent often." (Tirmidhi)

🕊 Dua: Ya Rahim, teach me to extend to myself the compassion You so freely give.

Day 19

Affirmation: Anger may visit, but it doesn't get to stay.

I used to let it camp out in my chest, replaying every offense. Now, I let it knock, speak, and leave without unpacking.

📖 Qur'an: "Repel evil with that which is better." (Surah Fussilat 41:34)

🕊 Dua: Ya Haleem, make me patient enough to release what doesn't serve my soul.

Day 20

Affirmation: I am worthy of gentleness, even from myself.

The voice in my head used to be crueler than anyone outside. I had to learn to talk to myself the way I talk to the people I love.

📖 Qur'an: "And lower your wing to the believers who follow you." (Surah Ash-Shu'ara 26:215)

🕊 Dua: Ya Wadud, teach me to love myself in the ways that please You.

Day 21

Affirmation: My story is not over. I get to write a new chapter.

I once believed this was all I'd ever be—angry, hurt, reactive. But healing taught me that I have permission to begin again.

📖 Qur'an: "Indeed, Allah will not change the condition of a people until they change what is in themselves." (Surah Ar-Ra'd 13:11)

🕊 Dua: Ya Mujib, help me to begin again with courage, and continue with consistency.

WEEK 4: Days 22–31

Day 22

Affirmation: I can start again without shame.

Each time I slipped back into anger, I thought I failed. But Allah allows us to begin again with every breath—and I'm learning to take those chances.

📖 Qur'an: "Do not despair of the mercy of Allah. Indeed, Allah forgives all sins." (Surah Az-Zumar 39:53)

🕊 Dua: Ya Ghaffar, cover my faults and open new doors with every new intention.

Day 23

Affirmation: My softness is a strength, not a flaw.

In survival mode, I built walls. But the strongest parts of me were always my compassion and tenderness. That's where my healing lives.

📖 Qur'an: "And We placed compassion and mercy in the hearts of those who followed him." (Surah Al-Hadid 57:27)

🕊 Dua: Ya Rahim, help me embrace my softness as part of my power.

Day 24

Affirmation: My heart belongs to the One who created it, not the one who broke it.

I gave pieces of myself to people who didn't value them. Now I return my heart to the One who always did.

📖 Qur'an: "And rely upon the Ever-Living who does not die." (Surah Al-Furqan 25:58)

🕊 Dua: Ya Quddus, purify my heart and make it whole again through Your nearness.

Day 25

Affirmation: My worth is not tied to my productivity.

On days when I could barely get out of bed, I felt useless. But Allah never asked me to prove my worth—only to remember it.

📖 Qur'an: "Indeed, the most noble of you in the sight of Allah is the most righteous of you." (Surah Al-Hujurat 49:13)

🕊 Dua: Ya Mughni, remind me that I am valuable just by being Yours.

Day 26

Affirmation: I am more than my reactions—I am my recovery.

I used to measure myself by how I failed to stay calm. Now, I celebrate how quickly I come back to myself—and to Allah.

📖 Hadith: "The one who repents from sin is like one who did not sin." (Ibn Majah)

🕊 Dua: Ya Tawwab, make my return to You faster than my fall into anger.

Day 27

Affirmation: I don't have to fight every battle—some things deserve my silence.

I thought if I didn't defend myself, I was weak. But silence has saved me more than my words ever have.

📖 Qur'an: "And be patient over what they say and avoid them with gracious avoidance." (Surah Al-Muzzammil 73:10)

🕊 Dua: Ya Jabbar, fight for me in the unseen and let my silence be a shield.

Day 28

Affirmation: My scars are signs that I've healed, not that I'm broken.

I tried to hide what I'd been through. Now, I wear my growth openly—proof that pain didn't win.

📖 Qur'an: "And He found you lost and guided [you]." (Surah Ad-Duhaa 93:7)

🕊 Dua: Ya Hadi, guide me from woundedness into wisdom.

Day 29

Affirmation: I let go of who I had to be in survival mode.

There was a version of me that didn't cry, didn't feel, didn't ask for help. She got me here. But she doesn't have to run the show anymore.

📖 Qur'an: "And He gives you from all you ask of Him." (Surah Ibrahim 14:34)

🕊 Dua: Ya Kareem, let me evolve into the woman You created me to be—whole, not hardened.

Day 30

Affirmation: I am allowed joy, even if I once knew only pain.

There was guilt the first time I smiled after grief. But joy is not betrayal—it's part of healing.

📖 Qur'an: "Say, in the bounty of Allah and in His mercy—in that let them rejoice." (Surah Yunus 10:58)

🤲 Dua: Ya Noor, fill my life with light after the darkness I've known.

Day 31

Affirmation: Every ending is a doorway to something sacred.

The end of that relationship, that season, even that version of me—it hurt. But Allah replaced each loss with something better. Sometimes, endings are divine.

📖 Qur'an: "It may be that you dislike a thing which is good for you." (Surah Al-Baqarah 2:216)

🤲 Dua: Ya Fattah, open doors for me I didn't know I needed, and close the ones that block my growth.

MONTH 2:

LOVE

*"Indeed, those who believe and do righteous deeds—
the Most Merciful will appoint for them affection."*
(Surah Maryam 19:96)

This month, we open to love—not just what we give or get, but the kind we grow within.

WEEK 1: Days 1–7

Day 1

Affirmation: Love starts with how I speak to myself.

I used to call myself names in my head that I'd never say to anyone else. Healing began when I replaced criticism with compassion.

📖 Qur'an: "And speak to people good [words]." (Surah Al-Baqarah 2:83)

🕊 Dua: Ya Wadud, teach me to speak to myself with the love You've always shown me.

Day 2

Affirmation: I am already loved by the One who made me.

No matter who left or betrayed me, the One who formed me never has. That truth steadies me.

📖 Qur'an: "Indeed, my Lord is Merciful and Affectionate." (Surah Hud 11:90)

🕊 Dua: Ya Rahman, let me feel Your love more deeply than the pain of my past.

Day 3

Affirmation: I do not need to earn love—I need to accept it.

I spent so long performing to feel worthy of affection. Now I know, real love doesn't demand exhaustion—it welcomes me as I am.

📖 Hadith: "None of you will enter Paradise by his deeds alone." They asked, "Not even you, O Messenger of Allah?" He said, "Not even me, unless Allah grants me His mercy." (Bukhari & Muslim)

🕊 Dua: Ya Rahim, open my heart to receive love without fear or striving.

Day 4

Affirmation: Love is not pain disguised as loyalty.

I stayed in relationships that hurt me, calling it patience. But Allah does not ask us to bleed for love—He asks us to honor it with truth.

📖 Qur'an: "And do not throw yourselves with your own hands into destruction." (Surah Al-Baqarah 2:195)

🤲 Dua: Ya Hakeem, help me recognize the difference between love and control.

Day 5

Affirmation: Love begins with boundaries, not sacrifice.

I thought love meant saying yes to everything. Now, I know boundaries are how I keep love honest, safe, and sacred.

📖 Hadith: "The strong believer is better and more beloved to Allah than the weak believer." (Muslim)

🤲 Dua: Ya Qawiyy, give me strength to protect my peace without guilt.

Day 6

Affirmation: Love grows where forgiveness lives.

Holding grudges drained me. But forgiving—especially myself—watered the seeds of peace I'd been longing for.

📖 Qur'an: "Let them pardon and overlook. Would you not like that Allah should forgive you?" (Surah An-Nur 24:22)

🤲 Dua: Ya Afuww, soften my heart so I can love without chains.

Day 7

Affirmation: I can love others without losing myself.

I used to pour from an empty cup, shrinking myself to fit someone else's needs. Now, I love from overflow, not depletion.

📖 Qur'an: "And do not forget your share of the world." (Surah Al-Qasas 28:77)

🕊️ Dua: Ya Malik, teach me to hold myself sacred even as I love those around me.

WEEK 2: Days 8–14

Day 8

Affirmation: The love I give myself teaches others how to love me.

Before I knew how to treat myself with care, I accepted carelessness from others. Now, I model the love I deserve by how I treat myself.

📖 Qur'an: "Indeed, Allah will not change the condition of a people until they change what is in themselves." (Surah Ar-Ra'd 13:11)

🕊️ Dua: Ya Allah, let my self-love reflect the value You've placed in me.

Day 9

Affirmation: Real love holds space for imperfection.

I thought I had to be perfect to be loved. But love rooted in fear of flaws isn't love at all—it's performance. Allah's love holds all of me.

📖 Hadith: "Every son of Adam sins, and the best of those who sin are those who repent." (Tirmidhi)

🕊️ Dua: Ya Ghafur, let me love others—and myself—with the same mercy You show me daily.

Day 10

Affirmation: I release the love that hurts more than it heals.

There were people I loved deeply who harmed me repeatedly. Holding on didn't make it love—it made it pain with a pretty name.

📖 Qur'an: "And We have not made the Qur'an difficult to remember. So is there any who will remember?" (Surah Al-Qamar 54:17)

🤲 Dua: Ya Fattah, open my eyes to love that honors, not harms.

Day 11

Affirmation: My heart heals faster in the presence of gentleness.

The people who helped me most weren't the loudest—they were the kindest. Gentleness is the soil where love takes root.

📖 Qur'an: "And by the mercy of Allah, you dealt with them gently." (Surah Aal Imran 3:159)

🤲 Dua: Ya Halim, place gentleness in my speech and actions so love can grow around me.

Day 12

Affirmation: I don't chase love—I attract it through truth.

I used to bend, shrink, and beg. But the love I was looking for began showing up the moment I started showing up for myself.

📖 Qur'an: "Verily, Allah loves those who rely upon Him." (Surah Aal Imran 3:159)

🤲 Dua: Ya Waliyy, let truth and trust draw the love that is meant for me.

Day 13

Affirmation: Every act of love brings me closer to Allah.

Whether it's smiling at a stranger or forgiving someone who hurt me, love in action is worship—and I'm reclaiming it daily.

📖 Hadith: "You will not enter Paradise until you believe, and you will not believe until you love one another." (Muslim)

🕊 Dua: Ya Wadud, make my love sincere and a means to grow nearer to You.

Day 14

Affirmation: I can be full of love and still walk away from what harms me.

Love doesn't mean staying where I'm unseen or unsafe. I can love deeply and still choose myself.

📖 Qur'an: "And do not let the hatred of a people prevent you from being just. Be just; that is nearer to righteousness." (Surah Al-Ma'idah 5:8)

🕊 Dua: Ya Adl, guide me to love that is just, and let me release what blocks my light.

WEEK 3: Days 15–21

Day 15

Affirmation: The more I love for Allah's sake, the freer I feel.

Loving for dunya drained me. Loving for Allah—expecting nothing in return—set me free from neediness and gave my heart rest.

📖 Hadith: "Whoever loves for Allah and hates for Allah... has completed his faith." (Abu Dawood)

🕊 Dua: Ya Allah, purify my intentions so my love is rooted in Your pleasure, not my ego.

Day 16

Affirmation: I can give love and still protect my heart.

I used to confuse openness with overexposure. But setting emotional limits doesn't mean withholding love—it means loving wisely.

📖 Qur'an: "And do not follow [your own] desire, as it will lead you astray." (Surah Sad 38:26)

🕊 Dua: Ya Hadi, guide my heart to love with strength and serenity.

Day 17

Affirmation: True love helps me grow, not shrink.

Real love cheers my growth, not my silence. Anyone who demands I dim my light doesn't deserve a front-row seat in my life.

📖 Qur'an: "And cooperate in righteousness and piety, but do not cooperate in sin and aggression." (Surah Al-Ma'idah 5:2)

🕊 Dua: Ya Samad, place in my life those who water my soul, not wither it.

Day 18

Affirmation: Love doesn't require me to be perfect—only present.

I was always trying to show up flawless, afraid love would leave if I slipped. But love rooted in Allah makes space for my humanity.

📖 Qur'an: "Allah intends for you ease and does not intend for you hardship." (Surah Al-Baqarah 2:185)

🕊 Dua: Ya Latif, teach me to be real over polished, and to be loved in truth.

Day 19

Affirmation: I let go of loving people who demand I abandon myself.

If I have to lose myself to be loved, it's not love—it's a performance. I now choose peace over pretense.

📖 Qur'an: "And do not obey the one whose heart We have made heedless of Our remembrance." (Surah Al-Kahf 18:28)

🕊 Dua: Ya Nur, light my path toward those who love me in alignment with You.

Day 20

Affirmation: Loving others starts with loving Allah most.

When I made people my center, I kept falling. When I placed Allah there, love became steady—not chaotic.

📖 Qur'an: "And those who believe are stronger in love for Allah." (Surah Al-Baqarah 2:165)

🕊 Dua: Ya Wadud, root me in divine love so I never settle for less than sacred.

Day 21

Affirmation: Love requires action, not just words.

I've heard 'I love you' from lips that wounded me. Now, I listen for love in consistency, in care, in character.

📖 Qur'an: "Say, [O Muhammad], 'If you should love Allah, then follow me, so Allah will love you.'" (Surah Aal Imran 3:31)

🕊 Dua: Ya Malik, teach me to love through action, not illusion.

WEEK 4: Days 22−28

Day 22

Affirmation: I release love that confuses chaos for passion.

For too long, I mistook drama for desire. But real love brings peace—not turbulence—and peace is what I now protect.

📖 Qur'an: "And it is He who created from water a human being and made him [a relative by] lineage and marriage. And your Lord is competent [concerning creation]." (Surah Al-Furqan 25:54)

🕊 Dua: Ya Salam, let the love I choose be calm, centered, and anchored in You.

Day 23

Affirmation: Love is not control dressed as care.

They said they were protecting me—but it was really about power. True love honors freedom and trusts without forcing.

📖 Qur'an: "There shall be no compulsion in [acceptance of] the religion." (Surah Al-Baqarah 2:256)

🕊 Dua: Ya Hakeem, grant me discernment to recognize control masked as care.

Day 24

Affirmation: I let go of anyone who loves my wounds more than my healing.

They liked me broken because I was easier to manage. But my healing exposed who was truly there for me—and who never was.

📖 Qur'an: "Say: The truth is from your Lord. Let him who will, believe, and let him who will, disbelieve." (Surah Al-Kahf 18:29)

🤲 Dua: Ya Shafi, surround me with those who celebrate my growth, not just my survival.

Day 25

Affirmation: I give love that uplifts, not one that enslaves.

Love should never be a cage. My heart now knows the difference between attachment that suffocates and connection that frees.

📖 Qur'an: "And hold firmly to the rope of Allah all together and do not become divided." (Surah Aal Imran 3:103)

🤲 Dua: Ya Rahman, bless me with connections that align with my soul and with You.

Day 26

Affirmation: I deserve love that does not make me question my worth.

If I'm constantly wondering if I'm enough, that's not love—it's emotional insecurity. Real love affirms without conditions.

📖 Qur'an: "And He has placed between you affection and mercy." (Surah Ar-Rum 30:21)

🤲 Dua: Ya Muqaddim, bring into my life the kind of love that lifts, not lowers me.

Day 27

Affirmation: I let my love be a reflection of my healing, not my hurt.

When I loved from wounds, I bled onto others. Now, I love from wholeness—and it feels like prayer, not punishment.

📖 Hadith: "The believer is not a fault-finder nor one who curses frequently, nor is he immoral or indecent." (Tirmidhi)

🤲 Dua: Ya Latif, refine my heart so my love reflects Your mercy, not my pain.

Day 28

Affirmation: Love rooted in faith never leads me astray.

I've followed hearts into heartbreak. But love that begins with Allah always leads me back to myself and to peace.

📖 Qur'an: "Indeed, those who have believed and done righteous deeds—the Most Merciful will appoint for them affection." (Surah Maryam 19:96)

🤲 Dua: Ya Wadud, let every love in my life begin and end with You.

MONTH 3:

AWARENESS

"And in yourselves—do you not see?"
(Surah Adh-Dhariyat 51:21)

This month is about noticing the inner world without judgment—
becoming conscious of what drives, calms, or ignites us.

WEEK 1: Days 1–7

Day 1

Affirmation: Awareness is the first step to change.

I used to explode in anger without understanding why. Learning to pause and notice what triggered me gave me power I didn't know I had.

Qur'an: "And do not follow that of which you have no knowledge. Indeed, the hearing, the sight, and the heart—about all those [one] will be questioned." (Surah Al-Isra 17:36)

Dua: Ya Basir, open my eyes to see myself clearly and respond with intention.

Day 2

Affirmation: My body tells the truth—awareness helps me listen.

Tight jaw. Racing heart. Shaking hands. My body always knew when I was upset before my words did. Now I listen and breathe before I react.

Qur'an: "And in yourselves. Then will you not see?" (Surah Adh-Dhariyat 51:21)

Dua: Ya Alim, increase me in awareness of what my body needs in moments of distress.

Day 3

Affirmation: I can hold space for my emotions without being ruled by them.

I used to run from my feelings or let them run me. Now, I acknowledge what I feel, but I let my values—not my mood—lead.

📖 Qur'an: "And those who avoid the major sins and immoralities, and when they are angry, they forgive." (Surah Ash-Shura 42:37)

🤲 Dua: Ya Halim, help me observe my emotions without becoming enslaved to them.

Day 4

Affirmation: Awareness helps me respond, not just react.

In the heat of the moment, I used to say things I regretted. Now, I take a breath. That pause is sacred. It's where my growth lives.

📖 Qur'an: "And speak to people good [words]." (Surah Al-Baqarah 2:83)

🤲 Dua: Ya Sabur, grant me patience in the pause so I may choose peace over regret.

Day 5

Affirmation: The more I understand my past, the more I control my future.

My triggers weren't random—they were echoes from old wounds. Healing started when I faced them, not when I ignored them.

📖 Qur'an: "Indeed, Allah will not change the condition of a people until they change what is in themselves." (Surah Ar-Ra'd 13:11)

🤲 Dua: Ya Mujib, help me unpack my past without judgment and with Your guidance.

Day 6

Affirmation: I give myself permission to feel everything without shame.

There were days I was so angry, I felt like a bad Muslim. But even the Prophet (ﷺ) experienced anger. The key is awareness and restraint, not denial.

📖 Hadith: "The strong is not the one who overcomes others by his strength, but the strong is the one who controls himself while in anger." (Bukhari)

🤲 Dua: Ya Rahman, wrap me in mercy as I navigate my emotional storms.

Day 7

Affirmation: Awareness is a form of worship when it brings me closer to Allah.

The more I became conscious of my habits, my thoughts, and my choices, the more I saw how much I needed Allah in everything.

📖 Qur'an: "And be not like those who forgot Allah, so He made them forget themselves." (Surah Al-Hashr 59:19)

🤲 Dua: Ya Dhikr, make me mindful of You in all I do, so that I may know myself through Your light.

WEEK 2: Days 8–14

Day 8

Affirmation: I can witness my thoughts without believing all of them.

Some days, my mind told me lies: 'You're too broken,' 'You're too much.' But I've learned to observe those thoughts—not obey them.

📖 Qur'an: "Indeed, the hearing, the sight, and the heart—about all those [one] will be questioned." (Surah Al-Isra 17:36)

Dua: Ya Haqq, let me recognize truth even in the noise of my own mind.

Day 9

Affirmation: I observe without judgment so I can grow with compassion.

I used to be my harshest critic. Now, I pause and ask, 'What do I need?' instead of 'What's wrong with me?' That shift is sacred.

Qur'an: "And We have certainly created man and know what his soul whispers to him." (Surah Qaf 50:16)

Dua: Ya Rahim, teach me to look at myself through Your lens of mercy.

Day 10

Affirmation: Being aware of my anger helps me master it.

Anger isn't evil. It's a signal. The danger lies in what I do with it. These days, I listen to it before I act on it.

Hadith: "Do not become angry." The man repeated his request and the Prophet replied, "Do not become angry." (Bukhari)

Dua: Ya Malik, help me control my anger instead of letting it control me.

Day 11

Affirmation: Awareness keeps me grounded in the present, not lost in the past.

I used to replay old wounds like a broken record. Awareness helped me stop the cycle and live in the now—not back then.

Qur'an: "So do not weaken and do not grieve, and you will be superior if you are [true] believers." (Surah Aal Imran 3:139)

Dua: Ya Salaam, help me release the past so I can meet today with peace.

Day 12

Affirmation: I notice my patterns so I can choose differently.

I kept ending up in the same painful situations. Once I became aware of my patterns, I found the power to change the script.

Qur'an: "And remind, for indeed, the reminder benefits the believers." (Surah Adh-Dhariyat 51:55)

Dua: Ya Latif, show me the subtle patterns I repeat, and guide me to better choices.

Day 13

Affirmation: The more aware I become, the less I blame others for my peace.

I used to wait for others to behave differently so I could feel better. Now, I focus on managing my energy, not controlling theirs.

Qur'an: "Indeed, Allah does not change the condition of a people until they change what is in themselves." (Surah Ar-Ra'd 13:11)

Dua: Ya Mujeeb, empower me to take ownership of my peace with dignity.

Day 14

Affirmation: Self-awareness is a gift that keeps me aligned with my purpose.

Knowing my triggers, my tendencies, and my talents has helped me say no to distractions and yes to divine alignment.

Qur'an: "And I did not create the jinn and mankind except to worship Me." (Surah Adh-Dhariyat 51:56)

Dua: Ya Hadi, lead me to live with intention rooted in Your purpose for me.

WEEK 3: Days 15–21

Day 15

Affirmation: Awareness teaches me that stillness is strength.

I once thought reacting fast meant I was in control. But real power came when I learned to be still and observe.

Qur'an: "And when you are greeted with a greeting, greet in return with what is better than it or [at least] return it [in a like manner]." (Surah An-Nisa 4:86)

Dua: Ya Sabur, strengthen my stillness and let awareness anchor me.

Day 16

Affirmation: I am aware of the energy I carry into every space.

Sometimes I brought tension into a room before anyone said a word. Now I ask myself, 'What am I bringing with me today?'

Qur'an: "Indeed, the mercy of Allah is near to the doers of good." (Surah Al-A'raf 7:56)

Dua: Ya Rahman, fill me with calm so I may be a source of peace to others.

Day 17

Affirmation: Awareness helps me find the lesson in every hardship.

Pain used to blind me. But when I leaned into awareness, even my anger became a teacher.

📖 Qur'an: "Perhaps you hate a thing and it is good for you." (Surah Al-Baqarah 2:216)

🕊 Dua: Ya Hakim, reveal the wisdom behind my struggles so I may grow from them.

Day 18

Affirmation: I can sit with discomfort without running from it.

I used to numb the discomfort—food, distractions, denial. Now I sit, breathe, and ask what the pain wants to teach me.

📖 Qur'an: "Verily, with hardship comes ease." (Surah Ash-Sharh 94:6)

🕊 Dua: Ya Qadir, help me remain present through discomfort until healing arrives.

Day 19

Affirmation: My awareness allows me to take responsibility, not shame.

I confused accountability with self-blame. But I've learned that awareness gives me power—not punishment.

📖 Qur'an: "And those who, when they commit an immorality or wrong themselves, remember Allah and seek forgiveness." (Surah Aal Imran 3:135)

🕊 Dua: Ya Tawwab, guide me in owning my actions with grace and growth.

Day 20

Affirmation: The more aware I become, the more empowered I feel.

Anger used to leave me feeling helpless. But self-awareness turned that fire into fuel for healing and strength.

📖 Qur'an: "Say, 'Nothing will ever befall us except what Allah has destined for us.'" (Surah At-Tawbah 9:51)

🕊️ Dua: Ya Aziz, make me strong through the light of awareness.

Day 21

Affirmation: Awareness makes space for joy even in difficult moments.

When I paid attention, I found small joys even in dark seasons—a warm cup of tea, a friend's smile, a peaceful breath.

📖 Qur'an: "Indeed, with hardship comes ease." (Surah Ash-Sharh 94:6)

🕊️ Dua: Ya Fattah, open my heart to the joys I often overlook in moments of pain.

WEEK 4: Days 22–31

Day 22

Affirmation: My triggers are messengers, not enemies.

Each time something set me off, I thought I was broken. Now I realize my triggers are signs—calling me to heal deeper.

📖 Qur'an: "And He found you lost and guided [you]." (Surah Ad-Duha 93:7)

🕊️ Dua: Ya Hadi, guide me to understand what my reactions are really telling me.

Day 23

Affirmation: I can be aware of what's wrong and still grateful for what's right.

I used to feel like I had to choose—either face my pain or count my blessings. But both can coexist. That's maturity.

Qur'an: "If you are grateful, I will surely increase you [in favor]." (Surah Ibrahim 14:7)

Dua: Ya Shakur, help me hold both joy and struggle with balance and grace.

Day 24

Affirmation: Awareness doesn't mean overthinking—it means understanding.

I thought awareness meant spiraling in self-doubt. But now I know it's clarity—not confusion—that true awareness brings.

Qur'an: "Indeed, in that are signs for a people who give thought." (Surah Az-Zumar 39:42)

Dua: Ya Nur, illuminate my thoughts so I may see myself with wisdom.

Day 25

Affirmation: I release shame that clouds my clarity.

Shame kept me in hiding. When I let it go, I could finally see myself fully—and start to heal openly.

Qur'an: "And [He] removed from you your burden." (Surah Ash-Sharh 94:2)

Dua: Ya Ghaffar, free me from shame and let awareness bring me compassion.

Day 26

Affirmation: I check in with myself before checking out on others.

Sometimes I snapped without realizing I was tired, overwhelmed, or hungry. Now I check in—emotionally and spiritually—first.

Qur'an: "And be moderate in your pace and lower your voice; indeed, the most disagreeable of sounds is the voice of donkeys." (Surah Luqman 31:19)

Dua: Ya Raqib, help me recognize when I need care so I can treat others with it too.

Day 27

Affirmation: The more I notice, the more I can navigate wisely.

I didn't know why certain patterns repeated until I started to notice them. That's when I could finally do something different.

Qur'an: "So take warning, O people of vision." (Surah Al-Hashr 59:2)

Dua: Ya Hakim, bless me with vision to see clearly and act wisely.

Day 28

Affirmation: I make time to reflect, because silence is sacred.

In constant noise, I couldn't hear my heart—or my Lord. Quiet reflection brought back a sense of closeness I was missing.

Qur'an: "Those who remember Allah while standing or sitting or [lying] on their sides and give thought to the creation of the heavens and the earth." (Surah Aal Imran 3:191)

Dua: Ya Dhikr, let my quiet moments become doorways to Your remembrance.

Day 29

Affirmation: I grow when I am honest with myself.

It was hard to admit when I was wrong. But awareness without honesty is just denial in disguise. Growth needs truth.

📖 Qur'an: "And do not conceal testimony, for whoever conceals it—his heart is indeed sinful." (Surah Al-Baqarah 2:283)

🤲 Dua: Ya Haqq, make me honest with myself, even when it's uncomfortable.

Day 30

Affirmation: I give myself credit for every moment of awareness I've gained.

I used to overlook my growth. But even catching myself before reacting is a win. Awareness is progress—not perfection.

📖 Qur'an: "So whoever does an atom's weight of good will see it." (Surah Az-Zalzalah 99:7)

🤲 Dua: Ya Karim, help me honor every small step I take toward consciousness.

Day 31

Affirmation: I am not who I was—and that awareness is powerful.

I look back at how I used to think and react, and I barely recognize myself. That awareness is proof: I'm healing.

📖 Qur'an: "And that there is not for man except that [good] for which he strives." (Surah An-Najm 53:39)

🤲 Dua: Ya Quddus, sanctify my growth and make me grateful for how far I've come.

MONTH 4:

ACKNOWLEDGEMENT

*"Say, 'It is Allah who saves you from it and from every distress;
then you still associate others with Him.'"*
(Surah Al-An'am 6:64)

This month, we pause to recognize our truth, our story, and our survival. We don't need to explain—just to acknowledge.

WEEK 1: Days 1–7

Day 1

Affirmation: I acknowledge my pain without letting it define me.

For years, I ran from my hurt, fearing that facing it meant surrendering to it. But acknowledgment gave me clarity—and power.

Qur'an: "Indeed, with hardship comes ease." (Surah Ash-Sharh 94:6)

Dua: Ya Shafi, allow me to face what hurts with the courage that comes from knowing You heal.

Day 2

Affirmation: What I name, I can tame.

Anger had so many faces in me—grief, shame, exhaustion. When I started naming what I felt, I finally started healing it.

Qur'an: "Say, 'The truth is from your Lord.'" (Surah Al-Kahf 18:29)

Dua: Ya Haqq, help me speak truth into what I feel so that healing can begin.

Day 3

Affirmation: Acknowledging my story is not weakness—it's wisdom.

I used to hide my past in shame. Now I own it with grace. My journey made me, and I no longer pretend it didn't happen.

Qur'an: "And He found you lost and guided [you]." (Surah Ad-Duha 93:7)

Dua: Ya Latif, help me honor the path I've walked and the strength I've gained from it.

Day 4

Affirmation: I acknowledge the parts of me I used to avoid.

Some parts of me were loud and angry, others scared and silent. I denied them out of fear. Now, I embrace them with love.

📖 Qur'an: "Indeed, the human being is clearly ungrateful." (Surah Al-Adiyat 100:6)

🤲 Dua: Ya Rahim, let me bring compassion to every part of myself, especially the ones I once rejected.

Day 5

Affirmation: My emotions are signals, not sins.

I thought anger made me a bad Muslim. But even the Prophet (ﷺ) felt anger—he just knew how to hold it with dignity.

📖 Hadith: "The strong is not the one who overcomes others by his strength, but the one who controls himself while in anger." (Bukhari)

🤲 Dua: Ya Haleem, give me wisdom to acknowledge and direct my emotions toward healing.

Day 6

Affirmation: I don't have to justify my pain to validate it.

I used to explain away my feelings to make others comfortable. Now I know—if I feel it, it matters.

📖 Qur'an: "And We have certainly created man and know what his soul whispers to him." (Surah Qaf 50:16)

🤲 Dua: Ya Samī', hear what I carry even when I can't say it aloud.

Day 7

Affirmation: I acknowledge where I am, without rushing where I wish to be.

I tried to leap over the hard parts, thinking healing was a race. But peace came when I embraced the process instead of speeding past it.

📖 Qur'an: "Allah does not burden a soul beyond that it can bear." (Surah Al-Baqarah 2:286)

🤲 Dua: Ya Sabur, bless me with patience as I accept this moment fully, knowing You are with me in it.

WEEK 2: Days 8–14

Day 8

Affirmation: I acknowledge my growth, even when no one else sees it.

There were days I wanted applause just for making it through. Now I understand—some victories are between me and Allah alone.

📖 Qur'an: "He knows what is [present] before them and what will be after them." (Surah Al-Baqarah 2:255)

🤲 Dua: Ya Latif, help me witness my own growth through Your gentle gaze.

Day 9

Affirmation: I accept the truth, even when it's uncomfortable.

Denial kept me stuck. But once I acknowledged the reality I was avoiding, I could finally move forward.

Qur'an: "And do not mix the truth with falsehood or conceal the truth while you know [it]." (Surah Al-Baqarah 2:42)

Dua: Ya Haqq, give me strength to accept what is true and guidance to respond to it wisely.

Day 10

Affirmation: I am learning to acknowledge my needs without apology.

For so long I ignored my own needs to keep the peace. Now I understand that peace includes me, too.

Qur'an: "And We have certainly honored the children of Adam." (Surah Al-Isra 17:70)

Dua: Ya Kareem, teach me to treat my needs with the dignity You've given me.

Day 11

Affirmation: Acknowledging my part is how I reclaim my power.

I spent years blaming others. But once I saw where I had power to choose differently, I felt free again.

Qur'an: "Whatever strikes you of disaster—it is for what your hands have earned—but He pardons much." (Surah Ash-Shura 42:30)

Dua: Ya Adl, help me be just with myself—owning my mistakes and learning from them.

Day 12

Affirmation: I can acknowledge the harm without becoming bitter.

I feared that admitting how much someone hurt me would break me. Instead, it freed me from pretending I was okay.

Qur'an: "Repel evil with that which is better." (Surah Fussilat 41:34)

Dua: Ya Jabbar, mend what was broken when I didn't feel safe to speak the truth.

Day 13

Affirmation: I can hold space for both gratitude and grief.

Some days I missed what I never got. But I've learned that grief doesn't cancel gratitude—it deepens it.

Qur'an: "Indeed, We created man from a drop of fluid to test him; so We made him hearing, seeing." (Surah Al-Insan 76:2)

Dua: Ya Rahman, allow me to hold both my joy and my sorrow in Your mercy.

Day 14

Affirmation: Acknowledging my feelings is the beginning of emotional freedom.

I suppressed so much for so long that I forgot how to feel. Giving myself permission to feel was my path back to myself.

Qur'an: "He created man. He taught him eloquence." (Surah Ar-Rahman 55:3-4)

Dua: Ya Fattah, open my heart to the full range of feelings You created me to carry.

WEEK 3: Days 15–21

Day 15

Affirmation: I acknowledge that healing is not linear—and that's okay.

Some days I feel like I'm back at square one. But healing isn't a straight road. It curves, dips, and still moves forward.

📖 Qur'an: "And it may be that you dislike a thing which is good for you." (Surah Al-Baqarah 2:216)

🤲 Dua: Ya Hakim, help me trust the process even when I can't see the outcome.

Day 16

Affirmation: My feelings are valid, even if others don't understand them.

People told me I was too emotional. But Allah made me sensitive for a reason. Now, I see that as a gift—not a flaw.

📖 Qur'an: "And We have already created man and know what his soul whispers to him." (Surah Qaf 50:16)

🤲 Dua: Ya Basir, see me in my truth even when the world misunderstands me.

Day 17

Affirmation: I can acknowledge my fear without letting it rule me.

Fear used to run the show in my life. Now I call it out, breathe through it, and act from faith, not fear.

📖 Qur'an: "Do not fear; indeed, I am with you both—I hear and I see." (Surah Ta-Ha 20:46)

🤲 Dua: Ya Mu'min, grant me the courage to walk through fear with Your protection.

Day 18

Affirmation: Acknowledging my anger shows I respect myself.

I used to suppress my anger to keep peace, but it would always explode later. Now I acknowledge it early and honor its message.

📖 Qur'an: "Those who restrain anger and who pardon the people—Allah loves the doers of good." (Surah Aal Imran 3:134)

🤲 Dua: Ya Salam, teach me to express my anger with honesty and peace.

Day 19

Affirmation: I am allowed to take up space with my truth.

I made myself small so others could be comfortable. But truth doesn't shrink—it stands. And I'm learning to stand with it.

📖 Qur'an: "And speak to people good [words]." (Surah Al-Baqarah 2:83)

🤲 Dua: Ya Wali, strengthen my voice and protect me as I stand in truth.

Day 20

Affirmation: I acknowledge my desire to be loved and seen—without shame.

Wanting love doesn't make me needy. It makes me human. Allah created me to connect—and I'm no longer ashamed of that need.

📖 Qur'an: "And He placed between you affection and mercy." (Surah Ar-Rum 30:21)

🤲 Dua: Ya Wadud, fulfill my longing for love with the sweetness of Your nearness.

Day 21

Affirmation: My acknowledgment of the truth is the beginning of my liberation.

Lies kept me trapped in cycles of pain. But truth—no matter how hard—broke the chains I couldn't see.

Qur'an: "And say, 'Truth has come, and falsehood has perished. Indeed, falsehood is bound to perish.'" (Surah Al-Isra 17:81)

Dua: Ya Fattah, open every door I need to walk through in order to live free.

WEEK 4: Days 22–30

Day 22

Affirmation: I acknowledge my boundaries as a form of self-respect.

I used to say yes when I meant no. I feared rejection. Now I realize that boundaries aren't barriers—they're bridges to peace.

Qur'an: "And do not walk upon the earth exultantly. Indeed, you will never tear the earth [apart]." (Surah Al-Isra 17:37)

Dua: Ya Muhaymin, protect the spaces I guard for my peace and well-being.

Day 23

Affirmation: I acknowledge when I need rest without guilt.

I ran on empty for too long, thinking it made me strong. But rest is not weakness—it's worship if done with intention.

Qur'an: "And We made your sleep [a means for] rest." (Surah An-Naba 78:9)

Dua: Ya Salaam, grant me restful peace when I pause, and renew me in Your mercy.

Day 24

Affirmation: Acknowledgment opens the door to accountability, not shame.

I thought owning my mistakes made me less worthy. But accountability gave me dignity—and control of my life again.

Qur'an: "Every soul will be (held) in pledge for its deeds." (Surah Al-Muddathir 74:38)

Dua: Ya Tawwab, help me take ownership with honesty and move forward with grace.

Day 25

Affirmation: I acknowledge that my healing affects generations.

When I broke a cycle in myself, I saw it ripple through my family. This work is sacred—and bigger than me.

Qur'an: "Indeed, Allah will not change the condition of a people until they change what is in themselves." (Surah Ar-Ra'd 13:11)

Dua: Ya Warith, let the healing You begin in me become legacy for those after me.

Day 26

Affirmation: I acknowledge my resilience without denying my wounds.

Being strong didn't mean I didn't hurt. I finally let myself admit, 'Yes, I survived. But it was hard—and it mattered.'

📖 Qur'an: "So verily, with the hardship, there is relief." (Surah Ash-Sharh 94:6)

🕊 Dua: Ya Jabbar, heal what broke in silence and honor the strength it took to survive.

Day 27

Affirmation: I am worthy of care, even when I'm not performing.

I tied my worth to what I did for others. Now I know I am valuable even when I'm still, quiet, or just being.

📖 Qur'an: "Indeed, the most noble of you in the sight of Allah is the most righteous of you." (Surah Al-Hujurat 49:13)

🕊 Dua: Ya Rahman, remind me that I am beloved simply because I am Yours.

Day 28

Affirmation: I acknowledge joy when it visits and let it stay awhile.

I used to brace for the next storm, even in calm. Now I let joy sink in without fear it will vanish tomorrow.

📖 Qur'an: "Say, 'In the bounty of Allah and in His mercy—in that let them rejoice.'" (Surah Yunus 10:58)

🕊 Dua: Ya Karim, expand my heart to receive joy without suspicion or fear.

Day 29

Affirmation: I acknowledge that I am still becoming—and that is beautiful.

Perfection used to trap me in shame. But I am a work in progress, and every step forward counts.

Qur'an: "And to your Lord is the finality." (Surah An-Najm 53:42)

Dua: Ya Badi', continue shaping me with Your divine artistry and care.

Day 30

Affirmation: I acknowledge Allah as the ultimate witness to my healing.

Even when no one else saw the tears or growth, I knew Allah did. That's what kept me going.

Qur'an: "Is not Allah sufficient for His Servant?" (Surah Az-Zumar 39:36)

Dua: Ya Shahid, be my witness and reward every unseen moment of transformation.

MONTH 5:

ACCEPTANCE

"Perhaps you dislike a thing and it is good for you.."
(Surah Al-Baqarah 2:216)

Acceptance doesn't mean approval. This month, we stop fighting what is, so we can breathe into what will be.

WEEK 1: Days 1–7

Day 1

Affirmation: I accept that I cannot control everything—and that's okay.

I used to think control kept me safe. But it was surrender that gave me peace. I'm learning to trust what I can't see.

  Qur'an: "And rely upon Allah; and sufficient is Allah as Disposer of affairs." (Surah Al-Ahzab 33:3)

  Dua: Ya Wakeel, help me trust Your plan when mine falls apart.

Day 2

Affirmation: I accept all parts of me—the light and the shadow.

I tried to hide my flaws to be loved. But healing came when I accepted every part of myself with compassion.

  Qur'an: "He created you and formed you and perfected your forms." (Surah Ghafir 40:64)

  Dua: Ya Musawwir, help me see beauty in every part of who You shaped me to be.

Day 3

Affirmation: Acceptance is not giving up—it's letting go of resistance.

I fought against reality so long it exhausted me. But when I accepted what was, I found space to heal and grow.

  Qur'an: "Perhaps you hate a thing and it is good for you." (Surah Al-Baqarah 2:216)

  Dua: Ya Latif, soften my heart to receive what You decree, even when I don't understand it.

Day 4

Affirmation: I accept the past without allowing it to define my future.

The past shaped me, but it doesn't own me. I've learned from it, and now I walk forward with freedom.

Qur'an: "And whoever repents and does righteousness—indeed, he turns to Allah with [accepted] repentance." (Surah Al-Furqan 25:71)

Dua: Ya Tawwab, turn my past into wisdom and my mistakes into mercy.

Day 5

Affirmation: I accept the emotions I feel without judgment.

I used to tell myself I was too much or too emotional. Now I realize that my feelings are valid, even when messy.

Qur'an: "And He is with you wherever you are." (Surah Al-Hadid 57:4)

Dua: Ya Rahman, meet me in my emotions with kindness and calm.

Day 6

Affirmation: I accept others for who they are, not who I want them to be.

I held on to disappointment expecting people to change. Peace came when I stopped trying to rewrite their story.

Qur'an: "No soul bears the burden of another." (Surah Al-An'am 6:164)

Dua: Ya Hadi, guide me to peace through acceptance of others as they are.

Day 7

Affirmation: I accept that I am still healing, and that healing takes time.

I used to rush my recovery, ashamed I wasn't 'over it' yet. But healing is not a deadline—it's a devotion.

📖 Qur'an: "So be patient. Indeed, the promise of Allah is truth." (Surah Ar-Rum 30:60)

🕊️ Dua: Ya Sabur, grant me patience with myself as I grow at the pace of grace.

WEEK 2: Days 8–14

Day 8

Affirmation: I accept my need for healing with tenderness, not shame.

I once saw needing help as weakness. Now I see it as strength—a signal that I value my well-being.

📖 Qur'an: "Indeed, man was created weak." (Surah An-Nisa 4:28)

🕊️ Dua: Ya Shafi, bless my vulnerability and wrap it in Your healing mercy.

Day 9

Affirmation: I accept that growth means letting go of what no longer serves me.

Old habits felt safe, even when they hurt me. Letting go was scary—until I realized it made space for better things.

📖 Qur'an: "And whoever puts his trust in Allah—then He is sufficient for him." (Surah At-Talaq 65:3)

Dua: Ya Mughni, release me from what weighs me down and fill me with what lifts me up.

Day 10

Affirmation: I accept myself as I am, while working toward who I'm becoming.

There's beauty in the 'in-between.' I no longer wait to love myself until I've 'arrived.' I love myself now, as I grow.

Qur'an: "He knows what is before them and what is after them." (Surah Taha 20:110)

Dua: Ya Alim, help me honor the version of me that's becoming with gentleness and grace.

Day 11

Affirmation: I accept Allah's mercy is greater than my mistakes.

I punished myself for sins I had already repented from. Now I trust that when Allah forgives, I can forgive myself too.

Qur'an: "Say, 'O My servants who have transgressed against themselves [by sinning], do not despair of the mercy of Allah.'" (Surah Az-Zumar 39:53)

Dua: Ya Rahim, teach me to see myself through the lens of Your mercy, not my guilt.

Day 12

Affirmation: I accept that forgiveness is a gift I give myself.

Holding onto resentment drained me. When I let it go, I realized forgiveness isn't always about them—it's about freeing me.

Qur'an: "But if you pardon and overlook and forgive—then indeed, Allah is Forgiving and Merciful." (Surah At-Taghabun 64:14)

Dua: Ya Ghaffar, show me the way to let go so I may live lighter and freer.

Day 13

Affirmation: I accept the lessons that came with my pain.

I used to ask, 'Why me?' Now I ask, 'What did this teach me?' That shift brought wisdom I never expected.

Qur'an: "And He found you lost and guided [you]." (Surah Ad-Duha 93:7)

Dua: Ya Hakeem, turn my wounds into wisdom and my struggles into strength.

Day 14

Affirmation: I accept that peace can exist alongside imperfection.

I thought I had to have everything in order before I could feel peace. But peace came when I welcomed life as it is.

Qur'an: "Indeed, in the remembrance of Allah do hearts find rest." (Surah Ar-Ra'd 13:28)

Dua: Ya Salaam, grant me peace that is not dependent on perfection, but anchored in You.

WEEK 3: Days 15–21

Day 15

Affirmation: I accept that I deserve compassion, even on my worst days.

There were days I felt I had nothing to offer. But even then, Allah's mercy never left. That's the model I now offer myself.

📖 Qur'an: "And My Mercy encompasses all things." (Surah Al-A'raf 7:156)

🕊️ Dua: Ya Rahman, cover me with compassion, especially when I struggle to extend it to myself.

Day 16

Affirmation: I accept that slowing down is part of my healing journey.

Pushing through the pain didn't make it go away—it buried it deeper. I'm learning that stillness is strength too.

📖 Qur'an: "And He it is who makes [you] laugh and weep." (Surah An-Najm 53:43)

🕊️ Dua: Ya Halim, teach me the power of pausing and the grace in going slow.

Day 17

Affirmation: I accept that boundaries protect my peace—not punish others.

I feared setting limits would push people away. But the right people respected my boundaries—and I gained peace.

📖 Qur'an: "And do not transgress. Indeed, Allah does not like transgressors." (Surah Al-Baqarah 2:190)

🕊 Dua: Ya Wali, help me guard what is sacred within me through respectful boundaries.

Day 18

Affirmation: I accept that I am not alone, even when I feel lonely.

In my loneliest moments, I remembered that Allah is always near. That truth became my anchor.

📖 Qur'an: "Indeed, I am near." (Surah Al-Baqarah 2:186)

🕊 Dua: Ya Qareeb, let me feel Your nearness when human comfort feels far away.

Day 19

Affirmation: I accept that grieving is not weakness—it's love in another form.

I used to hide my grief, afraid it made me seem fragile. But grieving showed me how deeply I had loved—and that's nothing to hide.

📖 Qur'an: "Do not grieve; indeed, Allah is with us." (Surah At-Tawbah 9:40)

🕊 Dua: Ya Jabar, soothe my aching heart and remind me You are with me in every tear.

Day 20

Affirmation: I accept the seasons of my life—each with its own wisdom.

I spent years fighting change. But with every season, Allah taught me something new about strength, patience, and surrender.

📖 Qur'an: "Indeed, with hardship comes ease." (Surah Ash-Sharh 94:6)

🕊 Dua: Ya Muqallib al-qulub, help me embrace each season of life with trust and grace.

Day 21

Affirmation: I accept that healing means being present with what is.

Wishing things were different kept me stuck. Now I anchor myself in the now—and that's where healing lives.

📖 Qur'an: "And you do not will except that Allah wills." (Surah At-Takwir 81:29)

🤲 Dua: Ya Malik al-Mulk, ground me in this moment and grant me peace in what is.

WEEK 4: Days 22–31

Day 22

Affirmation: I accept the limits of others without taking it personally.

I used to feel rejected when others couldn't show up how I needed. Now I see their limitations are not a reflection of my worth.

📖 Qur'an: "Each soul earns not [blame] except against itself." (Surah Al-An'am 6:164)

🤲 Dua: Ya Hakam, help me detach from what I cannot control and find peace in my own lane.

Day 23

Affirmation: I accept the pace of my healing—no matter how slow it feels.

I thought I had to heal fast to be okay. But slow healing has been deeper, truer, and more lasting than I imagined.

Qur'an: "And whoever is patient and forgives—indeed, that is of the matters [requiring] determination." (Surah Ash-Shura 42:43)

Dua: Ya Sabur, strengthen me with patience that leads to lasting peace.

Day 24

Affirmation: I accept discomfort as a signal, not an enemy.

Discomfort used to scare me. But now I see it as a message—a nudge toward growth, not punishment.

Qur'an: "Indeed, with hardship [will be] ease." (Surah Ash-Sharh 94:6)

Dua: Ya Wasi', help me stretch with grace and grow beyond fear.

Day 25

Affirmation: I accept that Allah knows what I do not.

When I couldn't make sense of the pain, I reminded myself: Allah's knowledge is complete. Mine is not. That brought surrender.

Qur'an: "And Allah knows, while you know not." (Surah Al-Baqarah 2:216)

Dua: Ya Aleem, guide me to trust what You know is best, even when I can't yet see it.

Day 26

Affirmation: I accept that choosing peace doesn't mean I'm weak.

I used to think I had to fight to prove my strength. But walking away with grace? That takes a different kind of power.

Qur'an: "And when the ignorant address them [harshly], they say [words of] peace." (Surah Al-Furqan 25:63)

♡ Dua: Ya Aziz, bless me with the strength to walk in peace, even when provoked.

Day 27

Affirmation: I accept that my story is still being written—and Allah is the best Author.

Even in chaos, I know the pen is in divine hands. That calms my anxiety about what's to come.

📖 Qur'an: "Indeed, We have created all things with predestination." (Surah Al-Qamar 54:49)

♡ Dua: Ya Majeed, write for me a story filled with mercy, meaning, and healing.

Day 28

Affirmation: I accept joy when it comes and trust it will return again.

I used to be afraid to enjoy happiness—it felt too fleeting. Now I let it in fully, knowing Allah is the Source and Sustainer.

📖 Qur'an: "Say: In the bounty of Allah and His mercy—in that let them rejoice." (Surah Yunus 10:58)

♡ Dua: Ya Wahhab, increase me in joy and let it stay rooted in Your grace.

Day 29

Affirmation: I accept that letting go is sometimes the most loving choice.

Holding on out of fear only hurt me more. Letting go was not failure—it was faith that better would come.

📖 Qur'an: "But perhaps you hate a thing and it is good for you." (Surah Al-Baqarah 2:216)

🤲 Dua: Ya Fattah, open my hands and heart to what You have next for me.

Day 30

Affirmation: I accept myself as worthy of love, as I am today.

I spent so long trying to earn love. But now I know—my worth is not up for debate. Allah created me with purpose and love.

📖 Qur'an: "Indeed, We have created man in the best of stature." (Surah At-Tin 95:4)

🤲 Dua: Ya Wadud, let me feel the warmth of Your love within myself each day.

Day 31

Affirmation: I accept the journey—and I honor how far I've come.

I used to only see how far I had to go. Now, I pause to honor the mountains I've already climbed—and thank Allah for every step.

📖 Qur'an: "And your Lord is going to give you, and you will be satisfied." (Surah Ad-Duha 93:5)

🤲 Dua: Ya Shakur, thank You for sustaining me this far. I accept the rest of the journey in Your care.

MONTH 6:

FORGIVENESS

*"Let them pardon and overlook.
Would you not love for Allah to forgive you?"*
(Surah An-Nur 24:22)

This month is a call to free ourselves—not for them, but for us.
Forgiveness is peace we choose to live in.

WEEK 1: Days 1–7

Day 1

Affirmation: I forgive myself for what I didn't know before I knew it.

I used to beat myself up for past choices. But growth means I know better now—and that means I can do better.

   Qur'an: "And say, 'My Lord, increase me in knowledge.'" (Surah Taha 20:114)

   Dua: Ya Aleem, let my past become a source of insight, not shame.

Day 2

Affirmation: I forgive others not because they deserve it, but because I deserve peace.

I carried anger like armor, but it only wore me down. Letting go gave me back my joy.

   Qur'an: "And let them pardon and overlook. Would you not like that Allah should forgive you?" (Surah An-Nur 24:22)

   Dua: Ya Ghaffar, teach me to forgive the way I long to be forgiven.

Day 3

Affirmation: I forgive without needing an apology to move forward.

I waited for words that never came. Then I realized—freedom isn't about what they say. It's about what I release.

   Qur'an: "Repel [evil] by that [deed] which is better." (Surah Fussilat 41:34)

   Dua: Ya Haleem, make my heart soft enough to let go, even when others can't own their harm.

Day 4

Affirmation: I forgive slowly, in layers, and that's okay.

Some wounds took time to form—and they'll take time to heal. I'm giving myself space to peel back the hurt, one breath at a time.

📖 Qur'an: "And be patient, for indeed, Allah does not allow to be lost the reward of those who do good." (Surah Hud 11:115)

🤲 Dua: Ya Sabur, walk with me through the slow, sacred journey of forgiving.

Day 5

Affirmation: I forgive myself for surviving in ways that no longer serve me.

I coped how I could when I didn't know better. Now I choose new tools—with love, not judgment.

📖 Qur'an: "Allah does not burden a soul beyond that it can bear." (Surah Al-Baqarah 2:286)

🤲 Dua: Ya Latif, be gentle with my tender heart as I unlearn what once protected me.

Day 6

Affirmation: I forgive those who wounded me and left me to heal alone.

They disappeared after the damage. But I didn't disappear—I rebuilt. That's what matters now.

📖 Qur'an: "Indeed, your Lord is vast in forgiveness." (Surah An-Najm 53:32)

🤲 Dua: Ya Afuww, widen my capacity to forgive so that I can make room for peace.

Day 7

Affirmation: I forgive without forgetting the lesson.

Forgiveness doesn't mean repeating cycles. I honor what I learned, and still choose to heal.

📖 Qur'an: "Take what is given freely, enjoin what is good, and turn away from the ignorant." (Surah Al-A'raf 7:199)

🤲 Dua: Ya Hakim, help me carry the wisdom without carrying the weight.

WEEK 2: Days 8–14

Day 8

Affirmation: I forgive to lighten my soul, not to excuse the harm.

Forgiveness isn't letting someone off the hook—it's unhooking myself from pain they no longer carry.

📖 Qur'an: "And whoever pardons and makes reconciliation, his reward is [due] from Allah." (Surah Ash-Shura 42:40)

🤲 Dua: Ya Raheem, soften my heart enough to let go, but strong enough to remember the lesson.

Day 9

Affirmation: I forgive myself for what I allowed when I didn't know I had options.

Looking back, I stayed in situations that hurt me. But back then, I thought love meant enduring pain. I know better now.

Qur'an: "Indeed, Allah loves those who rely upon Him." (Surah Al-Imran 3:159)

Dua: Ya Wakil, remind me of my strength and restore my self-respect with compassion.

Day 10

Affirmation: I forgive without needing the relationship to continue.

I used to think forgiveness meant reconnecting. But some peace requires distance. I can forgive and still walk away.

Qur'an: "And do not let the hatred of a people prevent you from being just." (Surah Al-Ma'idah 5:8)

Dua: Ya Adl, grant me balance between mercy and self-preservation.

Day 11

Affirmation: I forgive the parts of me still healing and not yet whole.

Some days I react from wounds I thought were healed. Instead of shame, I now offer myself understanding and redirection.

Qur'an: "Our Lord, do not impose blame upon us if we have forgotten or erred." (Surah Al-Baqarah 2:286)

Dua: Ya Tawwab, accept my efforts and renew my heart through each stumble.

Day 12

Affirmation: I forgive because bitterness weighs more than pain.

The pain was real. But holding onto bitterness only kept me bound. Forgiveness released me from the cycle.

Qur'an: "So forgive with gracious forgiveness." (Surah Al-Hijr 15:85)

🕊 Dua: Ya Salaam, let my soul be light with grace, not heavy with resentment.

Day 13

Affirmation: I forgive so my heart can be a home for peace, not a prison for anger.

When I let anger take up residence in my heart, it left no room for peace. Now I choose peace—on purpose.

📖 Qur'an: "And We removed whatever was in their breasts of resentment." (Surah Al-A'raf 7:43)

🕊 Dua: Ya Nur, cleanse my heart of resentment and make space for Your light.

Day 14

Affirmation: I forgive because my soul was not created to carry hate.

Hatred burned inside me, pretending to be protection. But it was destroying me. Forgiveness brought water to the fire.

📖 Qur'an: "The good deed and the bad deed are not equal. Repel [evil] by that [deed] which is better." (Surah Fussilat 41:34)

🕊 Dua: Ya Wadud, fill my heart with love where pain once lived.

WEEK 3: Days 15–21

Day 15

Affirmation: I forgive because I am worthy of peace, not punishment.

For years, I thought holding onto pain made me righteous. But it only made me tired. Peace is the reward I now claim.

Qur'an: "Whoever does righteousness—it is for his own soul." (Surah Al-Jathiyah 45:15)

Dua: Ya Rahman, let peace flow through me like a healing river, washing away what I no longer need.

Day 16

Affirmation: I forgive without denying what happened.

Forgiveness doesn't mean pretending it didn't hurt. It means I choose to release the grip it has on my heart.

Qur'an: "Indeed, your Lord is swift in penalty; but indeed, He is Forgiving and Merciful." (Surah Al-A'raf 7:167)

Dua: Ya Adheem, help me hold truth and mercy at the same time.

Day 17

Affirmation: I forgive because resentment has no place in my healing.

I used to replay every offense. It kept me stuck. Now I replay my growth. That's the only cycle I want to be caught in.

Qur'an: "And whoever forgives and makes reconciliation—his reward is from Allah." (Surah Ash-Shura 42:40)

Dua: Ya Kareem, reward me with a heart lightened by letting go.

Day 18

Affirmation: I forgive because I believe in the possibility of transformation.

People change. I've changed. If I want grace for my evolution, I must leave room for theirs.

Qur'an: "And it may be that you dislike a thing which is good for you." (Surah Al-Baqarah 2:216)

💚 Dua: Ya Hadi, guide me to see beyond this moment into the potential of mercy.

Day 19

Affirmation: I forgive even if the other person doesn't change.

Waiting for their apology held me hostage. Now I choose release, whether or not they ever change.

📖 Qur'an: "And let them pardon and overlook." (Surah An-Nur 24:22)

💚 Dua: Ya Ghaffar, free me from needing anyone else's change to claim my healing.

Day 20

Affirmation: I forgive because I trust Allah's justice more than my own revenge.

Revenge tempted me. But justice belongs to Allah. I trust Him more than I trust my pain.

📖 Qur'an: "Indeed, Allah commands justice and good conduct." (Surah An-Nahl 16:90)

💚 Dua: Ya Haqq, You are the Truth and the Just—carry what I no longer need to hold.

Day 21

Affirmation: I forgive because I want to be free—not right.

Winning the argument never brought peace. But walking away with grace gave me more than any victory ever did.

📖 Qur'an: "And when they hear ill speech, they turn away from it." (Surah Al-Qasas 28:55)

💚 Dua: Ya Fattah, open the doors of freedom where ego used to stand.

WEEK 4: Days 22–30

Day 22

Affirmation: I forgive without needing closure from others.

Some conversations never came. Some apologies were never offered. And yet, I found peace in moving forward without them.

📖 Qur'an: "Indeed, Allah loves those who rely upon Him." (Surah Al-Imran 3:159)

🕊 Dua: Ya Wakil, be the closure I never received from others. Let You be enough.

Day 23

Affirmation: I forgive because I value my energy more than my ego.

Fighting to prove I was right drained me. Now I choose my energy and inner calm over being right.

📖 Qur'an: "And speak to people good [words]." (Surah Al-Baqarah 2:83)

🕊 Dua: Ya Rauf, fill me with calm that makes arguments unnecessary.

Day 24

Affirmation: I forgive myself for who I had to be to survive.

Sometimes I hardened to get through the pain. Now I soften to let healing in. That's strength too.

📖 Qur'an: "And He found you lost and guided [you]." (Surah Ad-Duhaa 93:7)

🕊 Dua: Ya Hadi, guide me gently from survival to peace.

Day 25

Affirmation: I forgive even when I still feel hurt.

I used to wait for the pain to go away before forgiving. But sometimes, forgiveness is the medicine—not the reward.

Qur'an: "And endure patiently, your patience is not but through Allah." (Surah An-Nahl 16:127)

Dua: Ya Sabur, grant me the courage to forgive before the wound is gone.

Day 26

Affirmation: I forgive so I can face the mirror with love.

Bitterness showed up in my face—in my tone, in my body. Forgiveness brought softness back to my reflection.

Qur'an: "He has succeeded who purifies it." (Surah Ash-Shams 91:9)

Dua: Ya Quddus, purify my soul until I see myself with mercy.

Day 27

Affirmation: I forgive because Allah forgives me, over and over.

When I think of how often I fall short—and how often Allah forgives—I realize I can extend that mercy too.

Qur'an: "Indeed, Allah is ever Pardoning and Forgiving." (Surah An-Nisa 4:43)

Dua: Ya Afuww, as You erase my sins, help me erase the bitterness in my heart.

Day 28

Affirmation: I forgive to model grace for those who come after me.

If my daughter ever feels betrayed, I want her to know that healing is possible. I forgive so she learns how to rise too.

📖 Qur'an: "There has certainly been for you in the Messenger of Allah an excellent pattern." (Surah Al-Ahzab 33:21)

🕊️ Dua: Ya Warith, let my legacy be one of grace and emotional freedom.

Day 29

Affirmation: I forgive because anger is not my identity.

I used to lead with my rage. But I've learned that under the fire was a wound—and under the wound was a heart that wanted peace.

📖 Qur'an: "And [Allah] removed the rage from their hearts." (Surah At-Tawbah 9:15)

🕊️ Dua: Ya Mujib, answer the call of my soul to be whole again.

Day 30

Affirmation: I forgive so I can finally rest.

I stayed in fight mode for years. Forgiveness let me breathe, sleep, and live again. That's what I fought for all along.

📖 Qur'an: "He is the One who sent down tranquility into the hearts of the believers." (Surah Al-Fath 48:4)

🕊️ Dua: Ya Salaam, settle my soul into rest that only Your mercy makes possible.

MONTH 7:

UNDERSTANDING

"And He gave you hearing, sight, and hearts that you might give thanks."
(Surah An-Nahl 16:78)

Understanding is a gift of the heart. This month, we learn to look deeper—past offense, into intention and need.

WEEK 1: Days 1–7

Day 1

Affirmation: I seek to understand my anger before I try to silence it.

I used to shut my anger down fast. Now I ask it what it's trying to protect. Listening taught me more than suppressing ever did.

📖 Qur'an: "Do not follow that of which you have no knowledge. Indeed, the hearing, the sight and the heart—about all those [one] will be questioned." (Surah Al-Isra 17:36)

🕊 Dua: Ya Baseer, open my eyes to see what lies beneath my emotion.

Day 2

Affirmation: I seek understanding, not just reaction.

I used to respond in heat. Now I pause. I want to understand, not just explode. That's where power lives.

📖 Qur'an: "And when they hear ill speech, they turn away from it and say, 'For us are our deeds, and for you are your deeds.'" (Surah Al-Qasas 28:55)

🕊 Dua: Ya Haleem, grant me calm before the storm.

Day 3

Affirmation: I give myself permission to feel before I fix.

I was raised to be strong. But strength is also in feeling the whole truth. Now I sit with what rises up.

📖 Qur'an: "And it is He who created for you hearing and vision and hearts; little are you grateful." (Surah Al-Mu'minun 23:78)

Dua: Ya Rahman, allow me to hold space for myself with care and compassion.

Day 4

Affirmation: I understand that my anger is often grief in disguise.

When I looked closer, the rage I held came from the pain of being dismissed, overlooked, or unloved. It was grief all along.

Qur'an: "Say, 'Travel through the land and observe how He began creation.'" (Surah Al-Ankabut 29:20)

Dua: Ya Jabbar, mend the broken places where grief pretends to be fury.

Day 5

Affirmation: I seek to understand others without losing myself.

I used to over-empathize, to the point of self-abandonment. Now I listen with boundaries, not blame.

Qur'an: "Invite to the way of your Lord with wisdom and good instruction." (Surah An-Nahl 16:125)

Dua: Ya Hakeem, grant me wisdom to hold both truth and tenderness.

Day 6

Affirmation: I understand that triggers are messages, not enemies.

When I got triggered, I'd lash out. But now I pause and ask—what is this reminding me of? What still needs healing?

Qur'an: "And in yourselves—do you not see?" (Surah Adh-Dhariyat 51:21)

Dua: Ya Shafi, heal what still hurts so I no longer react from pain.

Day 7

Affirmation: I understand that growth is rarely comfortable, but always worth it.

Every uncomfortable moment taught me something. I wouldn't have chosen it, but I'm grateful for what it grew in me.

   Qur'an: "Indeed, with hardship [will be] ease." (Surah Ash-Sharh 94:6)

   Dua: Ya Latif, help me grow through the discomfort with grace.

WEEK 2: Days 8–14

Day 8

Affirmation: I understand that every emotion is valid, even when it's uncomfortable.

I used to shame myself for feeling angry or sad. Now I recognize every emotion as a signpost, not a flaw.

   Qur'an: "He created man, [And] taught him eloquence." (Surah Ar-Rahman 55:3–4)

   Dua: Ya Khaliq, allow me to honor the full range of what You created in me.

Day 9

Affirmation: I understand that peace takes effort, not just desire.

Wanting peace wasn't enough. I had to build it—brick by brick, choice by choice.

📖 Qur'an: "And Allah invites to the Home of Peace." (Surah Yunus 10:25)

🤲 Dua: Ya Salaam, teach me how to make peace a daily practice.

Day 10

Affirmation: I understand that I am not the same person I was when I got hurt.

I carried pain as if it was still happening. But I'm not that version of me anymore. I've grown—and healing honors that.

📖 Qur'an: "Indeed, Allah will not change the condition of a people until they change what is in themselves." (Surah Ar-Ra'd 13:11)

🤲 Dua: Ya Musawwir, reshape me into someone who sees her progress clearly.

Day 11

Affirmation: I understand that some silence is strength, not weakness.

I thought speaking up meant power. But sometimes, choosing not to engage took even more strength.

📖 Qur'an: "And when they pass by ill speech, they pass by with dignity." (Surah Al-Furqan 25:72)

🤲 Dua: Ya Aziz, strengthen my dignity through mindful silence.

Day 12

Affirmation: I understand the difference between setting boundaries and building walls.

I used to shut everyone out to feel safe. Now I set clear limits, rooted in self-respect, not fear.

📖 Qur'an: "And do not forget graciousness between you." (Surah Al-Baqarah 2:237)

🕊 Dua: Ya Hafidh, protect my peace without hardening my heart.

Day 13

Affirmation: I understand that my triggers are my responsibility to heal.

It's not their job to tiptoe—it's my job to unpack why I react the way I do. That's how I reclaim power.

📖 Qur'an: "Every soul will be (held) in pledge for its deeds." (Surah Al-Muddathir 74:38)

🕊 Dua: Ya Tawwab, help me take ownership of my healing journey.

Day 14

Affirmation: I understand that forgiveness begins with understanding.

I used to think forgiveness came first. But understanding helped me forgive—not excuse—the harm, but make peace with it.

📖 Qur'an: "...and reconcile between your brothers. And fear Allah that you may receive mercy." (Surah Al-Hujurat 49:10)

🕊 Dua: Ya Rahim, let understanding be the path to forgiveness in my heart.

WEEK 3: Days 15–21

Day 15

Affirmation: I understand that growth requires reflection, not just reaction.

Reacting was easy. Reflecting took courage. It forced me to face the truth within myself and choose a better way.

Qur'an: "Do they not reflect upon themselves?" (Surah Ar-Rum 30:8)

Dua: Ya Noor, illuminate the lessons I've been too distracted to see.

Day 16

Affirmation: I understand that clarity often comes after the storm.

Sometimes I didn't understand what was happening until it passed. Hindsight gave me the wisdom I couldn't access in the moment.

Qur'an: "Perhaps you hate a thing and it is good for you." (Surah Al-Baqarah 2:216)

Dua: Ya Fattah, open my heart to the wisdom hidden in my trials.

Day 17

Affirmation: I understand that healing doesn't erase the past—it transforms how I carry it.

The past still happened, but it doesn't define me. Healing changed its meaning from wound to wisdom.

Qur'an: "Allah intends for you ease and does not intend for you hardship." (Surah Al-Baqarah 2:185)

Dua: Ya Rauf, help me carry my story with compassion, not shame.

Day 18

Affirmation: I understand that my pain has purpose when I face it with faith.

The hardest chapters of my life became my greatest teachers. Faith turned suffering into growth.

Qur'an: "Indeed, with hardship [will be] ease." (Surah Ash-Sharh 94:6)

🕊 Dua: Ya Sabur, show me the meaning within my struggle.

Day 19

Affirmation: I understand that I can disagree without disrespect.

I used to think anger gave me permission to be harsh. But I can express truth with dignity—and still be heard.

📖 Qur'an: "And speak to him with gentle speech that perhaps he may be reminded or fear [Allah]." (Surah Taha 20:44)

🕊 Dua: Ya Haleem, teach me patience even when I feel provoked.

Day 20

Affirmation: I understand that seeking knowledge is a form of worship.

The more I learned about myself, my faith, and my emotions, the closer I felt to Allah. Understanding is sacred.

📖 Qur'an: "Say, 'Are those who know equal to those who do not know?'" (Surah Az-Zumar 39:9)

🕊 Dua: Ya Alim, bless me with knowledge that softens my heart and strengthens my character.

Day 21

Affirmation: I understand that emotional intelligence begins with self-honesty.

Before I could manage my emotions, I had to admit what I was feeling. That honesty was my first act of healing.

📖 Qur'an: "And be not like those who forgot Allah, so He made them forget themselves." (Surah Al-Hashr 59:19)

🕊 Dua: Ya Haqq, let truth anchor me in every emotional storm.

WEEK 4: Days 22–31

Day 22

Affirmation: I understand that making space for others doesn't mean shrinking myself.

I used to quiet my truth so others could be comfortable. Now I speak gently—but I speak.

    Qur'an: "And lower your wing to the believers who follow you." (Surah Ash-Shu'ara 26:215)

    Dua: Ya Wadud, help me love others without abandoning myself.

Day 23

Affirmation: I understand that clarity in relationships comes from clear communication.

I used to expect others to just know how I felt. Now, I express what I need with courage and calm.

    Qur'an: "Say to My servants to say that which is best." (Surah Al-Isra 17:53)

    Dua: Ya Mubin, make my words bridges—not weapons.

Day 24

Affirmation: I understand that anger often covers fear or hurt.

When I paused to ask myself, 'What's really going on?,' I found fear beneath the flames. Facing it changed everything.

    Qur'an: "And when they became angry, they forgave." (Surah Ash-Shura 42:37)

Dua: Ya Ghani, help me name my truth so I can heal what lies beneath it.

Day 25

Affirmation: I understand that it's okay to not have all the answers.

I thought understanding meant control. Now I know that surrendering what I can't explain is also wisdom.

Qur'an: "And Allah knows, while you know not." (Surah Al-Baqarah 2:216)

Dua: Ya Aleem, comfort me when clarity doesn't come quickly.

Day 26

Affirmation: I understand that presence is more healing than perfection.

I used to think I had to fix everything. Sometimes just showing up, whole and honest, brings the healing needed.

Qur'an: "Indeed, the best of people are those who benefit others." (Hadith – Daraqutni)

Dua: Ya Rahim, let me be present with myself and others with gentleness.

Day 27

Affirmation: I understand that sometimes I am the one who needs forgiveness.

As much as I've been hurt, I've hurt others too. Owning that brought me closer to humility—and to Allah.

Qur'an: "And seek forgiveness of your Lord. Indeed, He is ever Forgiving." (Surah Nuh 71:10)

Dua: Ya Ghaffar, forgive me for the harm I caused, known and unknown.

Day 28

Affirmation: I understand that boundaries protect love—they don't block it.

I used to think saying no meant I didn't care. Now I know it means I care enough to keep things healthy.

Qur'an: "And do not let the hatred of a people prevent you from being just." (Surah Al-Ma'idah 5:8)

Dua: Ya Adl, help me honor balance in how I love and protect.

Day 29

Affirmation: I understand that every part of me deserves compassion.

Even the angry, broken parts of me are still mine. When I embrace them, they start to heal.

Qur'an: "And We have certainly created man and know what his soul whispers to him." (Surah Qaf 50:16)

Dua: Ya Rahman, meet me in the places I've struggled to love within myself.

Day 30

Affirmation: I understand that I can start again as many times as I need to.

Healing isn't linear. Some days I slipped. Some days I soared. But every day, Allah let me start again.

Qur'an: "Indeed, good deeds erase bad deeds." (Surah Hud 11:114)

Dua: Ya Tawwab, let each new effort count toward my wholeness.

Day 31

Affirmation: I understand that everything I've been through led me here—for a reason.

Even what tried to destroy me became part of what saved me. Every piece belongs to the journey.

Qur'an: "And perhaps you dislike a thing and Allah makes therein much good." (Surah An-Nisa 4:19)

Dua: Ya Hakim, help me trust the wisdom in every step of my path.

MONTH 8:

FAITH

"*And whoever relies upon Allah—then He is sufficient for him.*"
(Surah At-Talaq 65:3)

This month, we stand in the unseen. We choose to believe in healing even before it arrives.

WEEK 1: Days 1–7

Day 1

Affirmation: I have faith that Allah sees what no one else does.

There were times I cried in silence, hoping someone would understand. My comfort came when I remembered Allah always sees.

📖 Qur'an: "Indeed, my Lord is near and responsive." (Surah Hud 11:61)

🕊 Dua: Ya Sami, hear what my heart cannot say out loud and respond with mercy.

Day 2

Affirmation: I have faith that my pain has a purpose.

I didn't go through what I went through for nothing. Faith helps me trust that even the pain is part of His plan.

📖 Qur'an: "Perhaps you hate a thing and it is good for you." (Surah Al-Baqarah 2:216)

🕊 Dua: Ya Hakim, help me see the wisdom in what I do not yet understand.

Day 3

Affirmation: I have faith that I am never alone.

When no one answered the phone, when I felt abandoned, I remembered: Allah is always with me. That made me stronger.

📖 Qur'an: "Indeed, Allah is with those who fear Him and those who are doers of good." (Surah An-Nahl 16:128)

🕊 Dua: Ya Wali, be my companion in the moments I feel most forgotten.

Day 4

Affirmation: I have faith that Allah is not done with me yet.

My mistakes used to make me feel unworthy. But faith reminds me that I am a work in progress—and Allah is still writing my story.

📖 Qur'an: "Despair not of the mercy of Allah. Indeed, Allah forgives all sins." (Surah Az-Zumar 39:53)

🕊 Dua: Ya Tawwab, rewrite my path with Your mercy at every turn.

Day 5

Affirmation: I have faith that healing is possible, even when it feels far away.

Some wounds felt permanent. But time, effort, and prayer softened them. Healing isn't fast, but it is real.

📖 Qur'an: "And when I am ill, it is He who cures me." (Surah Ash-Shu'ara 26:80)

🕊 Dua: Ya Shafi, heal what lingers beneath the surface.

Day 6

Affirmation: I have faith that every prayer counts—even the whispered ones.

I used to think my prayers had to be perfect. But the most broken du'as brought me the most peace.

📖 Qur'an: "Call upon Me; I will respond to you." (Surah Ghafir 40:60)

🕊 Dua: Ya Mujib, respond to the prayers I barely have words for.

Day 7

Affirmation: I have faith that what's meant for me will reach me.

I chased people and things I thought I needed. Faith helped me release that grip. What's mine will never miss me.

Qur'an: "What Allah has willed [for you] will come to you." (Surah Al-Ahzab 33:36)

Dua: Ya Razzaq, provide what is best for me—even when I don't know what to ask for.

WEEK 2: Days 8–14

Day 8

Affirmation: I have faith that delay is not denial.

I used to think unanswered prayers meant rejection. But Allah's timing proved better than mine every time.

Qur'an: "And your Lord is never forgetful." (Surah Maryam 19:64)

Dua: Ya Sabur, teach me patience when the wait feels long.

Day 9

Affirmation: I have faith that even small steps matter.

There were days when just getting out of bed felt like victory. I now honor the small wins—they are part of the climb.

Qur'an: "So whoever does an atom's weight of good will see it." (Surah Az-Zalzalah 99:7)

Dua: Ya Latif, make me gentle with myself as I grow.

Day 10

Affirmation: I have faith that Allah knows my heart better than I do.

Sometimes I don't know what to ask for. But I trust that Allah already knows what I need most.

Qur'an: "He knows what is in every heart." (Surah Al-Mulk 67:13)

Dua: Ya Alim, answer the prayers I haven't even spoken yet.

Day 11

Affirmation: I have faith that love begins with self-compassion.

I used to seek love from those who couldn't give it. Now, I know love starts with how I treat myself—with kindness.

Qur'an: "And We have certainly honored the children of Adam..." (Surah Al-Isra 17:70)

Dua: Ya Rahman, teach me to love myself in the way You love me.

Day 12

Affirmation: I have faith that every hardship has hidden gifts.

My anger was once a shield. But buried beneath it were lessons, strength, and a deeper connection to my faith.

Qur'an: "Indeed, with hardship [will be] ease." (Surah Ash-Sharh 94:6)

Dua: Ya Wahhab, open my eyes to the blessings wrapped in pain.

Day 13

Affirmation: I have faith that I can begin again, no matter how many times I fall.

I thought falling meant failure. But each return to Allah is a triumph. Tawbah is my restart button.

📖 Qur'an: "Indeed, Allah loves those who repent and purify themselves." (Surah Al-Baqarah 2:222)

🕊 Dua: Ya Tawwab, welcome me back every time I return to You.

Day 14

Affirmation: I have faith that I am stronger than my struggle.

The pain was real, but so is the strength that carried me through. Allah didn't leave me empty-handed.

📖 Qur'an: "Allah does not burden a soul beyond that it can bear." (Surah Al-Baqarah 2:286)

🕊 Dua: Ya Qawi, remind me of the strength You placed inside me.

WEEK 3: Days 15–21

Day 15

Affirmation: I have faith that storms pass and leave behind strength.

There were times I thought I wouldn't survive what I was going through. But I did. And I came out stronger.

📖 Qur'an: "Verily, after hardship comes ease." (Surah Ash-Sharh 94:5)

🕊 Dua: Ya Jalil, grant me strength that outlasts every storm.

Day 16

Affirmation: I have faith that Allah responds in the best way, not always the fastest.

I once prayed for something I thought I needed immediately. Later I realized the delay protected me.

Qur'an: "It may be that you dislike a thing which is good for you." (Surah Al-Baqarah 2:216)

Dua: Ya Hakim, help me trust the delay as a sign of Your wisdom.

Day 17

Affirmation: I have faith that Allah values my effort even when I fall short.

I didn't always get it right. But I kept trying—and that effort was part of my worship.

Qur'an: "And that there is not for man except that [good] for which he strives." (Surah An-Najm 53:39)

Dua: Ya Adl, accept my striving even when it is imperfect.

Day 18

Affirmation: I have faith that what's for me won't require me to betray myself.

I've learned that anything that asks me to lose myself isn't from Allah. Real blessings align with my truth.

Qur'an: "And do not kill yourselves [or one another]. Indeed, Allah is to you ever Merciful." (Surah An-Nisa 4:29)

Dua: Ya Hadi, guide me to what is mine—without harm to who I am.

Day 19

Affirmation: I have faith that healing is not forgetting—it's remembering differently.

I used to fear my past. Now, I remember it with peace. I survived. That's the part I hold on to.

📖 Qur'an: "And remember the favor of Allah upon you..." (Surah Al-Ma'idah 5:7)

🤲 Dua: Ya Shakur, help me honor how far I've come.

Day 20

Affirmation: I have faith that Allah will make a way, even when I see none.

When doors kept closing, I thought I'd run out of options. Then Allah opened one I didn't even know existed.

📖 Qur'an: "And whoever relies upon Allah—then He is sufficient for him." (Surah At-Talaq 65:3)

🤲 Dua: Ya Fattah, open the doors I cannot yet see.

Day 21

Affirmation: I have faith that I am already enough in Allah's eyes.

I kept trying to earn love and worthiness. Then I remembered—Allah already created me with value.

📖 Qur'an: "And We have certainly honored the children of Adam..." (Surah Al-Isra 17:70)

🤲 Dua: Ya Karim, help me see myself through Your generous gaze.

WEEK 4: Days 22–30

Day 22

Affirmation: I have faith that my tears are never wasted.

I used to hide my crying, thinking it made me weak. But every tear I shed was seen—and valued—by Allah.

Qur'an: "And they fall upon their faces weeping, and it increases them in humility." (Surah Al-Isra 17:109)

Dua: Ya Basir, witness the tears I cry in silence and comfort me through them.

Day 23

Affirmation: I have faith that mercy is greater than punishment.

Fear used to keep me from turning back to Allah. Now I know—His mercy outweighs His wrath.

Qur'an: "My mercy encompasses all things." (Surah Al-A'raf 7:156)

Dua: Ya Rahim, let Your mercy find me when I fall.

Day 24

Affirmation: I have faith that forgiveness begins with faith in myself.

Before I could forgive others, I had to believe that I, too, deserved forgiveness. That took the most faith of all.

Qur'an: "Indeed, Allah loves those who rely upon Him." (Surah Al-Imran 3:159)

Dua: Ya Ghaffar, help me forgive what I've struggled to forget—even in myself.

Day 25

Affirmation: I have faith that Allah strengthens the brokenhearted.

When I felt most shattered, faith became my glue. Allah didn't ignore my brokenness—He repaired it.

Qur'an: "Indeed, the help of Allah is near." (Surah Al-Baqarah 2:214)

Dua: Ya Jabbar, mend the places where my heart still aches.

Day 26

Affirmation: I have faith that I am more than what I've survived.

My trauma wasn't the end of me—it was part of my transformation. Allah brought meaning to the mess.

☐ Qur'an: "Say, 'Nothing will happen to us except what Allah has decreed for us.'" (Surah At-Tawbah 9:51)

🕊 Dua: Ya Wakil, carry what I can no longer hold.

Day 27

Affirmation: I have faith that my story still holds beauty.

The parts of my life I once wanted to erase now remind me how far I've come—and how good Allah has been.

☐ Qur'an: "Indeed, Allah is subtle with His servants." (Surah Ash-Shura 42:19)

🕊 Dua: Ya Latif, help me see the beauty in every page of my journey.

Day 28

Affirmation: I have faith that peace is possible, even when chaos surrounds me.

The world didn't calm down—but I did. Peace came when I surrendered the need to control it all.

☐ Qur'an: "Truly it is in the remembrance of Allah that hearts find rest." (Surah Ar-Ra'd 13:28)

🕊 Dua: Ya Salam, bring peace to my inner world when the outer one feels loud.

Day 29

Affirmation: I have faith that even my silence is a form of worship.

There were times when I had no words left. But in that quiet, I felt closest to Allah.

Qur'an: "And be patient over what they say and avoid them with gracious avoidance." (Surah Al-Muzzammil 73:10)

Dua: Ya Halim, let my silence speak devotion when words fall short.

Day 30

Affirmation: I have faith that every breath is another chance.

Each new day, each inhale, is a reminder: I am still here, and Allah has not given up on me.

Qur'an: "And it is He who gives life and causes death." (Surah Al-Mu'minun 23:80)

Dua: Ya Muhyi, breathe new life into my faith today.

MONTH 9:

TRUST

"He is the best disposer of affairs."
(Surah Al-Imran 3:173)

Trust is a decision we renew daily. This month, we release what weighs us down and lean on divine wisdom.

WEEK 1: Days 1–7

Day 1

Affirmation: I trust that Allah knows what I can handle—even when I doubt it.

There were moments I felt overwhelmed, but in hindsight, I grew in ways I never imagined.

    Qur'an: "Allah does not burden a soul beyond that it can bear." (Surah Al-Baqarah 2:286)

    Dua: Ya Qawi, give me the strength to meet every challenge with grace.

Day 2

Affirmation: I trust that setbacks are setups for something better.

What felt like rejection was really redirection. I needed time to see the bigger picture.

    Qur'an: "But they plan, and Allah plans. And Allah is the best of planners." (Surah Al-Anfal 8:30)

    Dua: Ya Hakim, guide me through disappointments with faith in Your plan.

Day 3

Affirmation: I trust that I am guided, even when I feel lost.

Even when I had no clarity, I kept moving forward. Looking back, I see Allah's hand in every step.

    Qur'an: "And whoever puts their trust in Allah—then He is sufficient for them." (Surah At-Talaq 65:3)

Dua: Ya Hadi, guide my steps even when I can't see the path.

Day 4

Affirmation: I trust that surrender brings more peace than control.

Trying to control everything wore me out. Letting go and letting Allah gave me the peace I craved.

Qur'an: "And rely upon the Ever-Living who does not die." (Surah Al-Furqan 25:58)

Dua: Ya Wakeel, I place it all in Your hands. Grant me peace in release.

Day 5

Affirmation: I trust that healing happens in layers, not all at once.

Some pain took years to soften. I now honor my process and trust that Allah is not rushing me.

Qur'an: "Indeed, your Lord is vast in forgiveness." (Surah An-Najm 53:32)

Dua: Ya Sabur, give me patience for my unfolding.

Day 6

Affirmation: I trust that every test has a purpose I may not see yet.

Some trials made no sense until I realized they brought me closer to Allah than comfort ever did.

Qur'an: "Perhaps you dislike something and it is good for you." (Surah Al-Baqarah 2:216)

Dua: Ya Noor, shine light on what I can't yet understand.

Day 7

Affirmation: I trust that I don't have to have it all figured out.

I used to feel ashamed for not knowing what to do. Now I know trusting Allah is more important than having all the answers.

📖 Qur'an: "And sufficient is your Lord as a guide and helper." (Surah Al-Furqan 25:31)

🕊️ Dua: Ya Kareem, walk me through the unknown with mercy and direction.

WEEK 2: Days 8–14

Day 8

Affirmation: I trust that distance from people can bring me closer to Allah.

When I felt isolated and rejected, I turned inward—and found Allah waiting there.

📖 Qur'an: "And We are closer to him than [his] jugular vein." (Surah Qaf 50:16)

🕊️ Dua: Ya Qareeb, be my closest companion when others turn away.

Day 9

Affirmation: I trust that no prayer goes unheard—even if unanswered.

Some of my du'as still haven't been answered the way I imagined—but I know they were heard.

📖 Qur'an: "Call upon Me; I will respond to you." (Surah Ghafir 40:60)

🕊️ Dua: Ya Mujib, count every whisper as a seed of hope.

Day 10

Affirmation: I trust that I am not behind—I'm on Allah's timeline.

Comparison used to steal my joy. Now I know my journey is divinely paced and personal.

Qur'an: "Indeed, your Lord is swift in penalty; but indeed, He is Forgiving and Merciful." (Surah Al-An'am 6:165)

Dua: Ya Mudabbir, arrange my life with perfect timing and care.

Day 11

Affirmation: I trust that being vulnerable is a form of courage, not weakness.

Letting people see my truth used to terrify me. But with trust in Allah, I can be real and still feel safe.

Qur'an: "So whoever believes in Allah—He will guide his heart." (Surah At-Taghabun 64:11)

Dua: Ya Hafeedh, protect me as I show up with honesty and heart.

Day 12

Affirmation: I trust that change doesn't mean failure—it means growth.

Each shift in my life felt like instability until I realized it was part of evolving into who I'm meant to be.

Qur'an: "Indeed, Allah will not change the condition of a people until they change what is in themselves." (Surah Ar-Ra'd 13:11)

Dua: Ya Badī, shape my changes into something beautiful.

Day 13

Affirmation: I trust that making peace with my past frees my future.

I kept dragging old pain into new days. Once I trusted Allah with it, I finally felt free.

📖 Qur'an: "And He found you lost and guided [you]." (Surah Ad-Duhaa 93:7)

🕊️ Dua: Ya Haadi, lead me forward by healing what's behind me.

Day 14

Affirmation: I trust that Allah's plan includes my happiness—not just hardship.

I used to brace for pain, expecting struggle. But Allah has gifted me joy too—I just had to believe I deserved it.

📖 Qur'an: "Say, 'In the bounty of Allah and in His mercy—in that let them rejoice.'" (Surah Yunus 10:58)

🕊️ Dua: Ya Wahaab, fill my days with reasons to smile and give thanks.

WEEK 3: Days 15–21

Day 15

Affirmation: I trust that what's meant for me will never miss me.

I used to chase what was never mine. Now I walk with faith, knowing Allah brings what belongs to me.

📖 Qur'an: "What is meant for you will reach you, even if it is beneath two mountains." (Hadith, authenticated in meaning)

🕊️ Dua: Ya Razzaq, provide what is written for me without hardship or harm.

Day 16

Affirmation: I trust that rest is part of the journey—not a detour.

I thought pausing meant falling behind. But rest renewed me and brought me closer to Allah's mercy.

📖 Qur'an: "And We made your sleep [a means for] rest." (Surah An-Naba 78:9)

🤲 Dua: Ya Rahman, teach me to value rest as a form of trust in You.

Day 17

Affirmation: I trust that my value isn't determined by my past.

My old mistakes haunted me until I accepted that Allah's forgiveness defines me—not my regrets.

📖 Qur'an: "Say, 'O My servants who have transgressed against themselves, do not despair of the mercy of Allah.'" (Surah Az-Zumar 39:53)

🤲 Dua: Ya Ghaffar, help me walk forward without shame holding me back.

Day 18

Affirmation: I trust that being misunderstood does not diminish my truth.

Not everyone saw me clearly, but Allah always did. That trust gave me peace when words failed.

📖 Qur'an: "Indeed, Allah knows what is [hidden] within the breasts." (Surah Al-Mulk 67:13)

🤲 Dua: Ya Aleem, be my witness when no one else understands.

Day 19

Affirmation: I trust that Allah is not done with me yet.

There were days I wanted to give up. But Allah kept sending signs that my story wasn't over.

📖 Qur'an: "And your Lord is going to give you, and you will be satisfied." (Surah Ad-Duhaa 93:5)

🤲 Dua: Ya Baqi, keep me going when I feel like quitting.

Day 20

Affirmation: I trust that every sacrifice made for Allah is rewarded.

Letting go of what hurt felt impossible. But when I did it for Allah, He gave me something greater in return.

📖 Qur'an: "Whoever fears Allah—He will make for him a way out." (Surah At-Talaq 65:2)

🤲 Dua: Ya Jalil, honor the sacrifices that only You have seen.

Day 21

Affirmation: I trust that Allah never wastes a sincere effort.

Even when I didn't see results right away, I kept going. That consistency became my healing.

📖 Qur'an: "Indeed, Allah does not allow the reward of those who do good to be lost." (Surah At-Tawbah 9:120)

🤲 Dua: Ya Shakur, accept the efforts I've made in faith, even the quiet ones.

WEEK 4: Days 22–30

Day 22

Affirmation: I trust that quiet progress is still progress.

Some days I didn't feel like I was growing—but looking back, I was always moving, even in silence.

Qur'an: "And it is He who has made you successors upon the earth…" (Surah Fatir 35:39)

Dua: Ya Latif, help me honor the growth happening beneath the surface.

Day 23

Affirmation: I trust that anger can teach me, not just hurt me.

I used to be afraid of my anger. Now I see it as a signal, a messenger—not a master.

Qur'an: "And those who restrain anger and who pardon the people—Allah loves the doers of good." (Surah Al-Imran 3:134)

Dua: Ya Haleem, help me respond to anger with wisdom and grace.

Day 24

Affirmation: I trust that grief doesn't mean I'm broken—it means I've loved.

The sadness was deep, but it came from a place of connection. Allah saw every tear and held my heart.

Qur'an: "Indeed, we belong to Allah, and indeed to Him we will return." (Surah Al-Baqarah 2:156)

Dua: Ya Jabar, bind the parts of me grief tried to shatter.

Day 25

Affirmation: I trust that my pain has a purpose beyond what I see.

Every hardship brought a lesson, a new version of me that only pain could teach into being.

📖 Qur'an: "And We will surely test you... But give good tidings to the patient." (Surah Al-Baqarah 2:155)

🕊️ Dua: Ya Sabur, walk with me through the lessons pain carries.

Day 26

Affirmation: I trust that setting boundaries honors both me and Allah.

When I started saying 'no' to what drained me, I was finally saying 'yes' to my healing.

📖 Qur'an: "Do not burden a soul beyond what it can bear." (Surah Al-Baqarah 2:286)

🕊️ Dua: Ya Hakim, give me the courage to protect my peace.

Day 27

Affirmation: I trust that I'm allowed to begin again.

Even after my worst moments, Allah still allowed me to rise, to try again, to rewrite the next page.

📖 Qur'an: "Except for those who repent, believe and do righteous work." (Surah Al-Furqan 25:70)

🕊️ Dua: Ya Tawwab, bless every fresh start with Your mercy.

Day 28

Affirmation: I trust that love rooted in Allah can't be shaken by fear.

When I stopped loving from fear and started loving from faith, everything changed—even how I loved myself.

📖 Qur'an: "The most merciful to the believers is Allah." (Surah Al-Ahzab 33:43)

🕊️ Dua: Ya Wadud, fill my love with sincerity and strength.

Day 29

Affirmation: I trust that the hardest steps are the most sacred.

The day I chose to leave what was breaking me, I trusted that Allah would carry what I couldn't.

📖 Qur'an: "Indeed, Allah is with those who fear Him and those who are doers of good." (Surah An-Nahl 16:128)

🕊️ Dua: Ya Mu'min, give me faith enough to walk away when it's time.

Day 30

Affirmation: I trust that the journey is holy—even when it's hard.

Healing is not linear, but every step, even the stumbles, are part of what Allah is shaping in me.

📖 Qur'an: "And We have certainly created man and We know what his soul whispers to him…" (Surah Qaf 50:16)

🕊️ Dua: Ya Khaliq, continue shaping me into who I'm meant to become.

MONTH 10:

WORTH

"We have certainly honored the children of Adam..."
(Surah Al-Isra 17:70)

This month reminds us: our worth is divine, not determined by others. We are already enough.

WEEK 1: Days 1–7

Day 1

Affirmation: I am worthy of healing, no matter how broken I feel.

There was a time I thought healing was for other people. Then I remembered: Allah is a Healer for *everyone* who turns to Him.

   Qur'an: "And when I am ill, it is He who cures me." (Surah Ash-Shu'ara 26:80)

   Dua: Ya Shafi, heal the wounds I've buried too deep to name.

Day 2

Affirmation: I am worthy of love that doesn't hurt to hold.

I once confused struggle with love. Now I know real love is mercy, not pain.

   Qur'an: "And He placed between you affection and mercy." (Surah Ar-Rum 30:21)

   Dua: Ya Wadud, show me what love looks like when it reflects You.

Day 3

Affirmation: I am worthy of setting boundaries without guilt.

Saying no used to feel like a betrayal. But protecting my peace is an act of faith, not selfishness.

   Qur'an: "And do not make your own hands contribute to your destruction." (Surah Al-Baqarah 2:195)

   Dua: Ya Hakim, help me guard what You have entrusted to me—myself.

Day 4

Affirmation: I am worthy of being spoken to with respect.

I stayed silent through disrespect, thinking it was humility. But even the Prophet (ﷺ) corrected with dignity.

Qur'an: "And speak to people good [words]." (Surah Al-Baqarah 2:83)

Dua: Ya Adl, let justice begin in how I allow myself to be treated.

Day 5

Affirmation: I am worthy of peace, not just survival.

I didn't just want to make it—I wanted to breathe. Peace isn't extra; it's necessary.

Qur'an: "He it is who sent down tranquility into the hearts of the believers." (Surah Al-Fath 48:4)

Dua: Ya Salam, settle my spirit and teach me to live, not just endure.

Day 6

Affirmation: I am worthy of second chances—even from myself.

Forgiving myself was the hardest part. But if Allah can forgive me, who am I to hold a grudge against myself?

Qur'an: "Indeed, Allah forgives all sins." (Surah Az-Zumar 39:53)

Dua: Ya Ghaffar, help me give myself the mercy You've already offered me.

Day 7

Affirmation: I am worthy of being chosen, not just tolerated.

For years I begged for crumbs. But Allah reminded me: I am not hard to love—I was just asking the wrong hearts.

Qur'an: "Indeed, the most noble of you in the sight of Allah is the most righteous of you." (Surah Al-Hujurat 49:13)

Dua: Ya Muqaddim, lead me toward relationships that reflect my worth in Your eyes.

WEEK 2: Days 8–14

Day 8

Affirmation: I am worthy of being seen, even in my mess.

I used to hide the parts of me that hurt. But Allah sees all of me—and still loves me.

Qur'an: "He knows what is [present] before them and what will be after them." (Surah Al-Baqarah 2:255)

Dua: Ya Basir, see me through eyes of compassion when I feel unseen.

Day 9

Affirmation: I am worthy of joy without explanation.

Sometimes I dimmed my happiness to make others comfortable. Now I let it shine—it's a blessing, not a burden.

Qur'an: "Say, 'In the bounty of Allah and in His mercy—in that let them rejoice.'" (Surah Yunus 10:58)

Dua: Ya Fattah, open the door to joy I don't feel guilty for having.

Day 10

Affirmation: I am worthy of growth, even if it's slow.

I rushed my healing like it had a deadline. But Allah is patient—and so can I be.

📖 Qur'an: "So be patient. Indeed, the promise of Allah is truth." (Surah Ar-Rum 30:60)

🕊 Dua: Ya Sabur, grow me gently in the direction of wholeness.

Day 11

Affirmation: I am worthy of belonging without having to shrink.

I used to change myself just to fit in. But the right space makes you feel whole, not small.

📖 Qur'an: "And We have certainly honored the children of Adam…" (Surah Al-Isra 17:70)

🕊 Dua: Ya Aziz, make me strong enough to stand fully in who I am.

Day 12

Affirmation: I am worthy of protecting my peace.

I don't owe anyone access to my mind or my energy. That's not selfish—it's stewardship.

📖 Qur'an: "And do not obey every worthless habitual swearer." (Surah Al-Qalam 68:10)

🕊 Dua: Ya Hafidh, protect the sanctuary of my spirit.

Day 13

Affirmation: I am worthy of receiving without earning.

Allah's mercy isn't based on merit—it's based on love. I can receive without proving my worth.

📖 Qur'an: "Indeed, Allah is the possessor of bounty for the people..." (Surah Al-Baqarah 2:243)

🕊 Dua: Ya Kareem, remind me that I am loved, not because of what I do, but who You are.

Day 14

Affirmation: I am worthy of being cared for the way I care for others.

I gave and gave until I was empty. But I learned: what I pour into others, I also deserve.

📖 Qur'an: "And those who give what they give while their hearts are fearful..." (Surah Al-Mu'minun 23:60)

🕊 Dua: Ya Rauf, send me care that replenishes me, not just drains me.

WEEK 3: Days 15–21

Day 15

Affirmation: I am worthy of being spoken to with gentleness.

Harshness left scars I didn't speak about. Now I know I can expect kindness and still be strong.

📖 Qur'an: "And speak to him with gentle speech that perhaps he may be reminded or fear [Allah]." (Surah Ta-Ha 20:44)

🕊 Dua: Ya Haleem, soften the voices around me and within me.

Day 16

Affirmation: I am worthy of being celebrated, not just tolerated.

I used to shrink when praised, afraid I didn't deserve it. Now I accept that joyfully—it honors Allah's work in me.

📖 Qur'an: "And as for the favor of your Lord, report [it]." (Surah Ad-Duhaa 93:11)

🤲 Dua: Ya Majeed, let me honor the light You placed within me.

Day 17

Affirmation: I am worthy of release from what burdens me.

Carrying pain felt noble until I realized letting go was just as brave. I can breathe again now.

📖 Qur'an: "And [He] removed from you your burden." (Surah Ash-Sharh 94:2)

🤲 Dua: Ya Rafi, lift from me what I no longer need to carry.

Day 18

Affirmation: I am worthy of compassion even when I fall short.

I held myself to impossible standards. Allah reminded me that mercy, not perfection, is the goal.

📖 Qur'an: "And My mercy encompasses all things." (Surah Al-A'raf 7:156)

🤲 Dua: Ya Rahim, help me speak to myself the way You speak to Your servants.

Day 19

Affirmation: I am worthy of space to grow at my own pace.

Some grew faster. Some healed louder. But Allah gave me a lane of my own, and it's enough.

Qur'an: "Indeed, your efforts are diverse." (Surah Al-Lail 92:4)

Dua: Ya Wasi', make room for my healing in a world that rushes everything.

Day 20

Affirmation: I am worthy of dreams that don't have to die with my past.

I thought I missed my window. But the sunrise proves daily that it's never too late.

Qur'an: "And it is He who begins creation; then He repeats it..." (Surah Yunus 10:4)

Dua: Ya Muhyi, breathe new life into the goals I buried.

Day 21

Affirmation: I am worthy of a soft life, not one shaped only by survival.

Hardship taught me strength, but I don't have to live in fight mode forever. Ease is also from Allah.

Qur'an: "Allah intends for you ease and does not intend for you hardship." (Surah Al-Baqarah 2:185)

Dua: Ya Lateef, let ease be part of my story, not just struggle.

WEEK 4: Days 22–30

Day 22

Affirmation: I am worthy of friendships that feel like home.

I used to settle for one-sided connections. But now, I crave bonds that nourish, not deplete.

Qur'an: "Close friends, that Day, will be enemies to each other, except for the righteous." (Surah Az-Zukhruf 43:67)

Dua: Ya Wali, bless me with companions who reflect Your mercy and light.

Day 23

Affirmation: I am worthy of asking for help without shame.

Independence was my shield, but it became a cage. I now believe asking is strength, not weakness.

Qur'an: "And cooperate in righteousness and piety..." (Surah Al-Ma'idah 5:2)

Dua: Ya Mugheeth, surround me with people who honor my vulnerability with care.

Day 24

Affirmation: I am worthy of rest, not just productivity.

Rest once felt like laziness. Now I know even the Prophet ﷺ took time to restore himself.

Qur'an: "And We made your sleep [a means for] rest." (Surah An-Naba 78:9)

Dua: Ya Rahman, teach me to rest as a form of trust in You.

Day 25

Affirmation: I am worthy of laughter and lightness.

My anger once made joy feel forbidden. But even the Prophet ﷺ smiled often—why shouldn't I?

Qur'an: "That you may not grieve over what has escaped you..." (Surah Al-Hadid 57:23)

Dua: Ya Nur, brighten my path with moments of joy and ease.

Day 26

Affirmation: I am worthy of intimacy that honors my soul.

I used to think physical closeness meant love. Now I crave emotional safety and sacred connection.

Qur'an: "They are clothing for you and you are clothing for them." (Surah Al-Baqarah 2:187)

Dua: Ya Lateef, guide me to connections that honor my spirit as much as my body.

Day 27

Affirmation: I am worthy of silence that heals, not isolates.

I've learned that silence can be sanctuary, not punishment. In stillness, I meet myself and my Lord.

Qur'an: "And remember your Lord much and exalt [Him] with praise in the evening and the morning." (Surah Al-Imran 3:41)

Dua: Ya Sami', let me find peace in quiet moments of reflection.

Day 28

Affirmation: I am worthy of saying no without guilt.

Every yes that cost me peace wasn't worth it. Saying no saved my spirit more than once.

Qur'an: "And do not follow [your own] desire, as it will lead you astray from the way of Allah." (Surah Sad 38:26)

Dua: Ya Haqq, strengthen my boundaries without shame or fear.

Day 29

Affirmation: I am worthy of peace with my past.

I carried shame like it was part of me. But the past is a chapter—not the whole book.

Qur'an: "Do not despair of the mercy of Allah. Indeed, Allah forgives all sins." (Surah Az-Zumar 39:53)

Dua: Ya Tawwab, help me forgive what I cannot forget.

Day 30

Affirmation: I am worthy—because Allah said I am.

I spent too long trying to prove it. But my worth isn't up for debate. It's divinely declared.

Qur'an: "We have certainly created man in the best of stature." (Surah At-Tin 95:4)

Dua: Ya Khaliq, remind me of my sacred design when doubt creeps in.

MONTH 11:

SERVICE

"And do good as Allāh has done good to you..."
(Surah Al-Qasas 28:77)

This month, we pour from overflow, not emptiness. Service becomes sacred when it begins with self-care.

WEEK 1: Days 1–7

Day 1

Affirmation: I serve others best when I'm not running on empty.

I used to give until I had nothing left. But empty cups don't pour—and self-care is part of service.

Qur'an: "And do not forget your share of the world." (Surah Al-Qasas 28:77)

Dua: Ya Razzaq, refill what I give so I can serve from wholeness, not depletion.

Day 2

Affirmation: My service is valuable, even when it's quiet.

I thought only loud, public acts counted. But kindness in secret carries the most weight with Allah.

Qur'an: "If you disclose your charitable expenditures, they are good; but if you conceal them... it is better for you." (Surah Al-Baqarah 2:271)

Dua: Ya Latif, let my quiet offerings reach You even when no one else sees.

Day 3

Affirmation: Service begins with intention, not perfection.

I delayed giving until I could do it 'right.' But sincerity, not scale, is what Allah looks for.

Qur'an: "Allah does not burden a soul beyond that it can bear..." (Surah Al-Baqarah 2:286)

🤲 Dua: Ya Alim, purify my intentions and accept my effort even when it feels small.

Day 4

Affirmation: My anger can become fuel for justice, not harm.

I once let rage consume me. Now I try to turn it into change—serving those who hurt like I did.

📖 Qur'an: "Indeed, Allah commands justice and good conduct..." (Surah An-Nahl 16:90)

🤲 Dua: Ya Adl, use my anger as a tool for restoration, not destruction.

Day 5

Affirmation: Service isn't about being needed—it's about being willing.

I served for validation until I realized real service asks nothing in return. It's worship.

📖 Qur'an: "We feed you only for the countenance of Allah. We wish not from you reward or gratitude." (Surah Al-Insan 76:9)

🤲 Dua: Ya Quddus, cleanse my heart of ego so my service reflects only You.

Day 6

Affirmation: I can serve by simply showing up with presence.

I thought I had to fix things to be helpful. But sometimes, being there is enough.

📖 Qur'an: "And lower to them the wing of humility out of mercy..." (Surah Al-Isra 17:24)

🤲 Dua: Ya Rahman, make me present and kind in moments when words fall short.

Day 7

Affirmation: Even my healing can serve others.

Telling my story helped someone else speak theirs. Healing is contagious—and that's a form of service too.

Qur'an: "And whoever saves one [life]—it is as if he had saved mankind entirely." (Surah Al-Ma'idah 5:32)

Dua: Ya Shafi, let my healing ripple into the lives of others who are still hurting.

WEEK 2: Days 8–14

Day 8

Affirmation: I serve best when I protect my peace.

I used to think service meant sacrificing myself. But true giving flows from balance, not burnout.

Qur'an: "And do not throw [yourselves] with your [own] hands into destruction." (Surah Al-Baqarah 2:195)

Dua: Ya Hakeem, teach me to serve without losing myself.

Day 9

Affirmation: My acts of service are seeds—I may not see the fruit, but Allah does.

Sometimes I felt unnoticed. But Allah sees the unseen labor, and that's enough.

Qur'an: "Indeed, Allah does not allow the reward of those who do good to be lost." (Surah At-Tawbah 9:120)

Dua: Ya Basir, see the sincerity behind my silent efforts.

Day 10

Affirmation: I can serve through listening, not just doing.

I wanted to fix everything. Then I learned: being present, hearing someone out, is holy too.

Qur'an: "So give good tidings to My servants who listen to speech and follow the best of it." (Surah Az-Zumar 39:17–18)

Dua: Ya Sami', make me a better listener—one who brings comfort by simply being there.

Day 11

Affirmation: Even in anger, I can choose to serve with integrity.

My anger used to make me sharp. Now I let it sharpen my purpose, not my tongue.

Qur'an: "Those who restrain anger and who pardon the people—and Allah loves the doers of good." (Surah Al-Imran 3:134)

Dua: Ya Ghaffar, help me serve with a heart that releases, not retaliates.

Day 12

Affirmation: Service can look like boundaries too.

Sometimes serving means saying no. Protecting peace can be an offering to others too.

Qur'an: "Say, 'Each works according to his manner...'" (Surah Al-Isra 17:84)

Dua: Ya Haqq, let me serve in ways that align with truth, not people-pleasing.

Day 13

Affirmation: I am not responsible for saving everyone.

Trying to save everyone drained me. I had to learn: I am a servant, not a savior.

📖 Qur'an: "You are not over them a controller." (Surah Al-Ghashiyah 88:22)

🕊️ Dua: Ya Rabb, help me release what isn't mine to carry.

Day 14

Affirmation: My healing is an offering to the world.

The more I healed, the more others found permission to do the same. Healing multiplies.

📖 Qur'an: "And whoever does righteous deeds… We will surely cause him to live a good life." (Surah An-Nahl 16:97)

🕊️ Dua: Ya Shafi, let my healing be a lantern in someone else's dark night.

WEEK 3: Days 15–21

Day 15

Affirmation: I serve best when I show up as myself, not who people expect me to be.

Pretending drained me. Being real connects deeper. I've learned my truth is my offering.

📖 Qur'an: "And be yourself with those who call upon their Lord…" (Surah Al-Kahf 18:28)

Dua: Ya Haqq, make my authenticity a source of connection and healing.

Day 16

Affirmation: I can serve by simply staying kind in the face of hostility.

When I chose kindness over snapping back, I saw power in patience. That, too, is service.

Qur'an: "Repel evil with that which is better…" (Surah Fussilat 41:34)

Dua: Ya Halim, give me calm in moments when I feel provoked.

Day 17

Affirmation: My story is someone else's survival guide.

Sharing my pain used to scare me. But once I did, someone said, 'I needed that.'

Qur'an: "And remind, for indeed, the reminder benefits the believers." (Surah Adh-Dhariyat 51:55)

Dua: Ya Wahhab, let my truth be a gift to someone who feels alone.

Day 18

Affirmation: Service includes showing up for my inner child.

No one taught me how to love the wounded little girl inside. Now, I'm learning—and that's holy too.

Qur'an: "Indeed, Allah does not change the condition of a people until they change what is in themselves." (Surah Ar-Ra'd 13:11)

Dua: Ya Jabbar, mend what was broken in my younger self with Your healing hand.

Day 19

Affirmation: I serve when I advocate for others, even when it's uncomfortable.

Silence used to feel safe. But injustice demands a voice—and I have one.

📖 Qur'an: "O you who have believed, be persistently standing firm in justice…" (Surah An-Nisa 4:135)

🕊 Dua: Ya Adl, give me courage to speak up with grace and power.

Day 20

Affirmation: Making people laugh is a form of service too.

I thought healing had to be serious. But a shared laugh has saved more days than I can count.

📖 Qur'an: "And He it is who makes [one] laugh and weep." (Surah An-Najm 53:43)

🕊 Dua: Ya Fattah, open my heart to joy that heals.

Day 21

Affirmation: Sometimes rest is the most radical service I can offer.

Rest isn't retreat—it's strategy. Even the Prophet ﷺ paused. I'm learning to do the same.

📖 Qur'an: "So when you have finished [your duties], then stand up [for worship]." (Surah Ash-Sharh 94:7)

🕊 Dua: Ya Rafi', elevate my rest as devotion, not laziness.

WEEK 4: Days 22–30

Day 22

Affirmation: Letting others serve me is also an act of humility.

I always wanted to be the helper. But receiving with grace taught me that I'm not alone.

    Qur'an: "And cooperate in righteousness and piety..." (Surah Al-Ma'idah 5:2)

    Dua: Ya Wali, let me accept help with the same heart I offer it.

Day 23

Affirmation: The way I treat strangers reflects my devotion.

I used to reserve my best self for people I knew. Now I try to show up with kindness for everyone.

    Qur'an: "Say kind words to people..." (Surah Al-Baqarah 2:83)

    Dua: Ya Karim, let my everyday interactions be rooted in dignity and mercy.

Day 24

Affirmation: Grief can be sacred service when shared honestly.

My sadness once isolated me. But letting others witness it has brought unexpected healing.

    Qur'an: "And be patient over what befalls you..." (Surah Luqman 31:17)

    Dua: Ya Sabur, help me hold space for my sorrow and others' too.

Day 25

Affirmation: The most radical service is love without conditions.

I used to give expecting something back. True service expects nothing but reward from Allah.

Qur'an: "And they give food in spite of love for it to the needy..." (Surah Al-Insan 76:8)

Dua: Ya Wadud, teach me to love as You love—generously, without strings.

Day 26

Affirmation: My smile can be charity.

There were days I had little else to give. A smile still mattered. It softened the world.

Qur'an: "And speak to people good [words]..." (Surah Al-Baqarah 2:83)

Dua: Ya Nur, let joy flow from my face even when my heart is still healing.

Day 27

Affirmation: Honesty is a service to myself and others.

Truth was once painful to share. But truth delivered with compassion is a mercy.

Qur'an: "And do not mix the truth with falsehood or conceal the truth while you know [it]." (Surah Al-Baqarah 2:42)

Dua: Ya Haqq, let truth pour from me with kindness, not cruelty.

Day 28

Affirmation: Walking away from harm is a service to future generations.

Breaking cycles doesn't always feel noble—it's hard. But healing now saves those who come after me.

    Qur'an: "Indeed, Allah does not like transgressors." (Surah Al-Baqarah 2:190)

    Dua: Ya Qawiyy, strengthen me to build what I never received.

Day 29

Affirmation: Forgiveness is a service, even when I'm still hurting.

I thought forgiving meant forgetting. But I've learned it's about freeing myself to move forward.

    Qur'an: "But if you pardon and overlook and forgive—then indeed, Allah is Forgiving and Merciful." (Surah At-Taghabun 64:14)

    Dua: Ya Ghaffar, let me forgive without losing my boundaries.

Day 30

Affirmation: My life itself is service—every moment can be worship.

Whether I'm working, resting, laughing, or weeping—if I intend it for Allah, it becomes sacred.

    Qur'an: "Say, 'Indeed, my prayer, my rites of sacrifice, my living and my dying are for Allah…'" (Surah Al-An'am 6:162)

    Dua: Ya Rabb, make my whole life a testament of love and service to You.

MONTH 12:

PEACE

"O soul at peace, return to your Lord..."
(Surah Al-Fajr 89:27–28)

This final month is about calm resolve. We finish what we started—
with grace, gentleness, and gratitude.

WEEK 1: Days 1–7

Day 1

Affirmation: Peace is my birthright, not a reward I must earn.

I once believed I had to be perfect to feel peace. Now I know I can claim it as I am.

📖 Qur'an: "He will guide them and amend their condition and admit them to Paradise… peace." (Surah Muhammad 47:5–6)

🕊 Dua: Ya Salaam, wrap me in the peace that comes from knowing I am already enough.

Day 2

Affirmation: I create peace by not needing to control everything.

I used to grip life too tightly. Letting go made room for serenity to flow in.

📖 Qur'an: "And rely upon Allah; and sufficient is Allah as Disposer of affairs." (Surah Al-Ahzab 33:3)

🕊 Dua: Ya Wakeel, help me release what is not mine to manage.

Day 3

Affirmation: My anger does not disqualify me from peace.

There was a time I felt too broken to feel peace. But peace is a process, not a prize.

📖 Qur'an: "Indeed, the mercy of Allah is near to the doers of good." (Surah Al-A'raf 7:56)

🕊 Dua: Ya Rahim, meet me in the middle of my struggle and lead me gently to peace.

Day 4

Affirmation: My peace grows when I speak truth with love.

I used to silence myself to avoid conflict. But real peace is built on honest communication.

📖 Qur'an: "And speak to them noble words." (Surah Al-Isra 17:23)

🕊 Dua: Ya Haqq, guide my words to be both truthful and tender.

Day 5

Affirmation: Peace is found in the pauses.

Rushing kept me anxious. Pausing—before reacting, before deciding—became a gateway to calm.

📖 Qur'an: "So be patient with gracious patience." (Surah Al-Ma'arij 70:5)

🕊 Dua: Ya Sabur, teach me to find peace in stillness and patience in the pause.

Day 6

Affirmation: Forgiveness is a pathway to peace within.

Holding onto resentment made my soul heavy. Forgiveness became my release and refuge.

📖 Qur'an: "And let them pardon and overlook. Would you not like that Allah should forgive you?" (Surah An-Nur 24:22)

🕊 Dua: Ya Ghaffar, soften my heart to forgive others as You forgive me.

Day 7

Affirmation: Peace is choosing to stay grounded in the storm.

Life didn't stop throwing chaos my way. I just stopped giving it all my power.

Qur'an: "Verily, in the remembrance of Allah do hearts find rest." (Surah Ar-Ra'd 13:28)

Dua: Ya Majeed, anchor me in Your remembrance when everything else feels uncertain.

WEEK 2: Days 8–14

Day 8

Affirmation: I protect my peace by setting healthy limits.

I used to let everyone in. Now I guard my space with grace, not guilt.

Qur'an: "And do not follow your own desire lest you be unjust." (Surah Sad 38:26)

Dua: Ya Hadi, guide me to create boundaries that honor both others and myself.

Day 9

Affirmation: I choose peace over proving a point.

There's strength in walking away. I don't need to win arguments to feel worthy.

Qur'an: "And when the ignorant address them harshly, they say [words of] peace." (Surah Al-Furqan 25:63)

Dua: Ya Aziz, grant me dignity in silence and peace in surrender.

Day 10

Affirmation: My inner peace is not dependent on outside validation.

I chased approval until I learned that real peace is an inside job, not a popularity contest.

Qur'an: "Is it not sufficient for your Lord that He is, over all things, a Witness?" (Surah Fussilat 41:53)

Dua: Ya Shahid, let Your awareness of me be enough when others don't understand.

Day 11

Affirmation: Peace means releasing what I cannot change.

I fought reality for years. Peace found me when I stopped resisting and started trusting.

Qur'an: "Perhaps you hate a thing and it is good for you..." (Surah Al-Baqarah 2:216)

Dua: Ya Latif, help me surrender with softness instead of struggle.

Day 12

Affirmation: Joy and peace can coexist with my pain.

I thought healing had to mean constant happiness. Now I know peace allows for all emotions.

Qur'an: "So truly where there is hardship there is also ease." (Surah Ash-Sharh 94:6)

Dua: Ya Nur, shine light into my heart where both sorrow and sweetness reside.

Day 13

Affirmation: I have the right to protect my peace without explaining it.

Overexplaining drained me. I've learned that 'no' can be a complete sentence.

Qur'an: "And say, 'The truth is from your Lord, so whoever wills—let him believe.'" (Surah Al-Kahf 18:29)

Dua: Ya Malik, affirm my right to protect what You gave me—my peace.

Day 14

Affirmation: Peace grows when I accept who I am today.

I was waiting to be better before I gave myself peace. Now I claim it as I grow.

Qur'an: "Indeed, those who have said, 'Our Lord is Allah' and then remained steadfast…" (Surah Fussilat 41:30)

Dua: Ya Sabit, root me in the peace that comes from being present with myself.

WEEK 3: Days 15–21

Day 15

Affirmation: Peace lives in gratitude, not perfection.

I used to obsess over what was missing. When I started appreciating what was present, peace followed.

Qur'an: "If you are grateful, I will surely increase you [in favor]." (Surah Ibrahim 14:7)

Dua: Ya Shakur, open my heart to see the blessings that have always been there.

Day 16

Affirmation: Responding with gentleness is a radical act of peace.

I used to match people's energy. Now I choose gentleness—not to be weak, but wise.

📖 Qur'an: "And speak to him with gentle speech that perhaps he may be reminded..." (Surah Ta-Ha 20:44)

🕊️ Dua: Ya Haleem, fill my spirit with calm when others test my limits.

Day 17

Affirmation: My inner world deserves protection like sacred ground.

I gave people access to my peace who hadn't earned it. Now I treat my soul like sanctuary.

📖 Qur'an: "Do not follow that of which you have no knowledge..." (Surah Al-Isra 17:36)

🕊️ Dua: Ya Hadi, guide me to guard my peace with intention and wisdom.

Day 18

Affirmation: Surrendering to Allah is the deepest form of peace.

The day I stopped fighting what Allah had written, I discovered what real peace feels like.

📖 Qur'an: "He is the one who sent down tranquility into the hearts of the believers..." (Surah Al-Fath 48:4)

🕊️ Dua: Ya Mutakabbir, calm my ego so my soul can submit.

Day 19

Affirmation: Slowing down is not failure—it is faith in divine timing.

I rushed through life fearing I'd fall behind. But peace came when I aligned with divine pace.

Qur'an: "Indeed, your Lord is not unaware of what you do." (Surah Hud 11:123)

Dua: Ya Hakim, teach me to trust the timing of everything You've planned for me.

Day 20

Affirmation: Silence can be a sanctuary for the soul.

In the quiet, I met myself. In the stillness, I heard my Lord. Silence became sacred.

Qur'an: "...and remember your Lord within yourself in humility and in fear..." (Surah Al-A'raf 7:205)

Dua: Ya Samad, fill the silence with Your presence and my soul with Your peace.

Day 21

Affirmation: Releasing resentment opens the heart to peace.

I clung to old wounds like armor. Releasing them didn't make me weak—it made me whole.

Qur'an: "And We removed whatever was in their breasts of resentment..." (Surah Al-A'raf 7:43)

Dua: Ya Quddus, purify my heart from what weighs it down so I can rise in peace.

WEEK 4: Days 22–30

Day 22

Affirmation: Peace isn't always quiet—sometimes it roars with conviction.

I found peace not just in silence, but in standing firmly in my values without apology.

Qur'an: "O you who have believed, be persistently standing firm for Allah…" (Surah An-Nisa 4:135)

Dua: Ya Qawiyy, give me peace that stands strong even in resistance.

Day 23

Affirmation: I can be at peace even when others are in conflict.

There was a time I absorbed everyone's chaos. Now, I create space between their storm and my stillness.

Qur'an: "And when they hear ill speech, they turn away from it…" (Surah Al-Qasas 28:55)

Dua: Ya Hafiz, protect my spirit from chaos that isn't mine to carry.

Day 24

Affirmation: Peace begins with acceptance, not agreement.

I don't have to agree with everything to be at peace with it. Acceptance gave me room to breathe.

Qur'an: "To you be your religion, and to me my religion." (Surah Al-Kafirun 109:6)

Dua: Ya Wasi', widen my heart to accept what is beyond my control.

Day 25

Affirmation: Peace deepens when I release shame.

Shame kept me stuck in the past. But Allah's mercy invited me forward into peace.

📖 Qur'an: "Despair not of the mercy of Allah. Indeed, Allah forgives all sins..." (Surah Az-Zumar 39:53)

🕊️ Dua: Ya Tawwab, let Your forgiveness lift the weight of shame from my soul.

Day 26

Affirmation: Even in grief, peace can hold me.

Loss hollowed me, but peace found its way in—not by erasing pain, but by resting beside it.

📖 Qur'an: "Every soul will taste death... and We test you with evil and with good as trial..." (Surah Al-Anbiya 21:35)

🕊️ Dua: Ya Rahman, cradle my grief in the softness of Your mercy.

Day 27

Affirmation: Peace is a practice, not a destination.

I thought peace was a place to arrive. But now I know—it's something I return to again and again.

📖 Qur'an: "So whoever Allah wants to guide—He expands his breast to [contain] Islam..." (Surah Al-An'am 6:125)

🕊️ Dua: Ya Hadi, keep guiding me back to peace, no matter how far I stray.

Day 28

Affirmation: The presence of Allah is my greatest source of peace.

When people disappointed me, His nearness filled the void. It is in His presence that I truly rest.

> Qur'an: "Indeed, my Lord is near and responsive." (Surah Hud 11:61)

> Dua: Ya Mujib, remind me I am never alone when I am near to You.

Day 29

Affirmation: I have permission to protect my peace at all costs.

I used to feel guilty for saying no. Now I say it with peace and power.

> Qur'an: "And do not let the hatred of a people prevent you from being just..." (Surah Al-Ma'idah 5:8)

> Dua: Ya Adl, anchor me in fairness to myself as well as others.

Day 30

Affirmation: Living in peace is an act of worship.

Each breath I take in calm surrender is a form of remembrance. My peace is a prayer in motion.

> Qur'an: "O soul at peace, return to your Lord, well-pleased and pleasing [to Him]." (Surah Al-Fajr 89:27–28)

> Dua: Ya Salaam, let my life echo the peace I seek in death.

About the Author

'Aminah' Lynnette Anderson is a behavior specialist, emotional intelligence educator, and lifelong student of Islamic healing. With over 20 years of experience guiding individuals through anger, trauma, and self-awareness, she combines spiritual principles with psychological insight to create safe spaces for reflection and growth.

Aminah is a mother, grandmother, and writer whose work honors the complexity of emotion in the Muslim experience. She believes healing begins with honesty, continues through dhikr, and becomes whole through compassion.

Tame the Fire is her offering to every soul seeking peace through presence and faith through feeling.

www.ingramcontent.com/pod-product-compliance
Lightning Source LLC
Chambersburg PA
CBHW052220090526
44585CB00015BA/1260